The Man Who Worried

The Man Who Worried

John M. Drickamer

NORTHWESTERN PUBLISHING HOUSE
Milwaukee, Wisconsin

Library of Congress Card 87-62731
Northwestern Publishing House
1250 N. 113th St., P. O. Box 26975, Milwaukee, WI 53226-0975
©1987 by Northwestern Publishing House
Published 1988
Printed in the United States of America
ISBN 0-8100-0280-9

CONTENTS

1. ■ The Man Who Worried About the End

Read Luke 21:25-36; Matthew 24:3-41

There was a man named Fred, who liked to read science fiction books. One night in bed he was reading a new novel about the sun exploding and destroying the earth. As the people in the novel were expecting this horrendous event and were trying to escape in their space ships, one of the characters quoted Luke 21:25,26: "And there shall be signs in the sun, and in the moon, and in the stars; and upon the earth distress of nations, with perplexity; the sea and the waves roaring; Men's hearts failing them for fear, and for looking after those things which are coming on the earth: for the powers of heaven shall be shaken."

That night Fred had a terrible nightmare about the end of the world. It especially troubled him that the Bible could be quoted in the latest horror story. Fred did not sleep well the rest of the night. But the next day he forced himself to go to his job, without saying anything to his family or co-workers about this new worry.

That evening Fred was very silent at home, brooding over the problem. He decided to try to forget about it by watching television. First he watched the news. There was news about wars and rumors of wars. Then there was news about earthquakes in various parts of the world and people dying in burning buildings.

Fred was even more upset. So he turned to a talk show and heard a famous scientist talking about the universe. Fred thought, "At last I'll get some straight information!" The scientist talked about the history of the universe as he viewed it. Then he made some predictions. He said that the sun would eventually turn into a nova or a super-nova and make life in the solar system impossible. People would have to escape from this part of the universe sometime in the next million years or so.

Fred tried to find comfort in the idea that it was going to be a long time in the future. "By that time I'll be long dead, so I don't have to worry," he told himself. But somehow the thought of his own death did not cheer him up.

Fred switched the channel to a religious show. This show was advertised as making people feel real good, but what Fred heard made him worry more and more. There was a very excitable preacher talking about the end of the world and how it was just around the corner. He claimed that he had talked to an angel and had the latest interpretation of some Bible passage or other. He now knew for sure that the world was going to end in three months, no more.

So he said that there were only ninety days left in which to become more godly, more like Christ. There were only ninety days left in which to do enough good works, love enough people enough, give enough to the poor and needy — only ninety days left in which to rack up enough points on God's scoresheet to be counted among the saved on the day when Jesus would come back.

Fred was so upset that he spilled his beer all over the rug in the television room. Just as his wife Leona was commenting that it made the room smell like a brewery, the doorbell rang. Leona went to the door, and, of all people, it was Pastor Martin from their church.

Leona flirted with the idea of saying the beer smell was really just their shampoo. She decided not to say anything but simply to hope that he would not notice. She excused herself to tidy up and left Fred in the living room with the pastor.

Fred and Pastor Martin chatted for a while. Before the pastor said anything about it, Fred began to make some not very convincing excuses for not having been in church for a couple of months. Then he decided to ask the pastor about the end of the world. He said, "Pastor, I've been worried lately about the end of the world, about when Jesus is going to come again, and about what's going to happen when he does. When is he going to come anyway?"

Pastor Martin replied, "We don't know when Jesus is coming again. We can't know. The Bible says in so many words that no one but God knows that date in advance. It says that we are not to believe people who claim to know. The last day, according to the Bible, will come suddenly, unexpectedly, like a thief in the night."

"But doesn't the Bible say there will be signs we can see?" Fred asked.

"Fred", the pastor responded, "every time you are sick, that is a sign that you will die some day, but it does not tell you when you will die. In the same way, all the wars and rumors of wars, the earthquakes and other disasters keep reminding and warning us that the end is coming, but they do not tell us how soon it will come."

Fred went on, "But this book I was reading quoted the Bible about some signs that will tell us the end is real near."

Pastor Martin pulled out his pocket New Testament and thumbed in it for a minute. Then he read: "There shall be signs in the sun, and in the moon, and in the stars; and upon the earth distress of nations, with perplexity; the sea and the waves roaring; men's hearts failing them for fear, and for looking after those things which are coming on the earth: for the powers of heaven shall be shaken. And then shall they see the Son of man coming in a cloud with power and great glory. And when these things begin to come to pass, then look up, and lift up your heads; for your redemption draweth nigh" (Luke 21:25-28).

"Exactly!" said Fred. "That tells us we can know when it is going to happen."

"Not really," Pastor Martin replied. "It says that when the end of the world begins to happen, then we will know that it is happening. When the heavens and earth begin to be done away with, then we will know that Jesus is coming right away. It says, 'Then shall they see the Son of man.' When the end comes, everyone will know that it is happening, but no one will know in advance."

So Fred suggested hopefully, "Then we could have quite a bit of time yet."

The pastor answered, "We don't know. It could be a long time, or it could be a short time. It could be a thousand years from now, or it could be tonight."

Fred got quite upset and said, "But how can we get ready for it if we don't know when it's going to happen?"

Pastor Martin said, "We have to be ready all the time. We have to carry out our responsibilities on this earth just as if we knew that Christ was not coming back for a thousand years. But we have to be ready for him to come at any time. The Bible tells us to watch and be ready. Besides, even if Christ does not come back for many years, we could die at any time."

Fred said, "So we have to do what this television preacher said. We have to do lots of good works so that we can be ready and God will take us to heaven in case Christ comes back or in case we die in a car accident tomorrow. I read in the Bible, maybe it was in that same chapter, that we have to be considered worthy to escape punishment. Doesn't that mean that we have to do lots of good works in order to be ready for the end?"

4

Pastor Martin asked, "That idea worries you a great deal, doesn't it?"

Fred replied, "You betcha! I know I'm not ready. I haven't been the worst person in the world, but I haven't been the best either. I mean, I've got a few sins I'm gonna have to make up for. And I'm gonna have to start giving lots of money to the church and the poor, start being nicer to the wife and the kids, start being more honest at work. And, Pastor, I just don't know if I can do all that. I'm certain I can't do enough to make God happy with me."

"You can't do any good works on your own," the pastor said. "And you can't make up for your sins. You'll never get to heaven that way. The Bible says, 'By the works of the law shall no flesh be justified' (Galatians 2:16). None of us will be declared 'not guilty' on judgment day because of the good works we have done."

"I know that," Fred admitted, "so do I have any hope?"

"Yes, you do, Fred," the pastor quickly assured him. "God's word gives you hope. Our own works will not make us worthy to stand before Jesus, but there is a way. Christ's first coming takes away our worries about his second coming."

"What do you mean?" asked Fred.

Pastor Martin went on, "Because of the first coming of Christ we can happily and eagerly look forward to his second coming. I'll tell you why.

"Long ago the eternal Son of God came into this world by being born of a virgin mother. The same Jesus who was born at Bethlehem will come in the clouds with power and glory at the end of time.

"He came the first time to save us, not to judge us. That meant that he had to live the perfect, sinless life that we could not live. He did that for us and in our place. Then he took upon himself the guilt and punishment for all our sins, your sins and mine, Fred. He suffered and died on the cross of Calvary to pay the price for your sins and mine and those of the whole world. Now we can be happy about the end of

5

the world. Christ came the first time to make us eager for him to come the second time.

"Christ's life and death and resurrection mean the forgiveness of our sins. Now we are accounted worthy to stand before the Son of Man on the last day. Those who do not believe in him should be scared of judgment day. When Christ comes, they *will* be terrified. But those who do believe in him and in the forgiveness of sins he made real by his sacrifice on the cross, they will have nothing but joy and peace on judgment day. That will not be because of any good works of their own but because of Christ's good works for them. Believers do good works because God motivates them to love him and their fellow man, but they do not count on their good works to get them safely through judgment day. They count on Christ and on him alone."

"But how can I believe that? How can I know that it's true?" Fred asked.

Pastor Martin said, "It does sound too good to be true. But it's God's word, God's good word about his gracious will for us. We can't believe that by human thinking or trying. But God's power is in those words, and God uses this power to bring us to faith in Jesus our Savior. Our sins are forgiven for Jesus' sake, and God promises us eternal salvation. We can count on him to keep his promises."

Fred said, "You know, I'm not as worried about all this as I was a while ago. But I need to hear more."

The pastor said, "Even the weakest faith trusts that judgment day will be a good day for all believers in Christ, but you will need to hear this over and over again so that your faith will be nourished and strengthened and not die out."

2 The Man Who Worried About Death

Read Matthew 2:13-23

Fred had been a delinquent member of a Lutheran congregation. He had begun to worry about the end of the world. After Pastor Martin stopped to visit him and answered some of his questions on the basis of the Bible, Fred and his family started going to church again. They went every Sunday. When Advent came, they went to the Wednesday evening services. The children participated in the Christmas program. The family went to church on Christmas Eve and Christmas Day, and they all agreed that it was the best Christmas they had spent together.

Then on New Year's Eve tragedy struck the family. The youngest child, a boy, was killed by a hit and run driver. They never found out who it was, but it was probably someone who started celebrating early and was already drunk late in the afternoon. It was a terrible tragedy. It was a horrible thing to happen over the holidays — or anytime.

7

Imagine how the family felt! The other children were going through their first experience of the death of someone close to them. They were confused and sad. The winter sports equipment they had been given for Christmas went unused for the longest time. Fred's wife Leona cried a lot. Fred tried to be a tower of strength for his family. But "still waters run deep." Even though he did not show his emotions very much, he grieved as much as anyone else. It was terribly hard to end the old year with a death in the family and to begin the new year with a funeral. It was especially difficult when they looked at that small child's casket.

On Sunday they were in church again. As they listened to the pastor read the Gospel lesson, he came to the verse: "In Rama was there a voice heard . . . Rachel weeping for her children, and would not be comforted, because they are not" (Matthew 2:18). Leona wept openly at that point. It was understandable that she could not concentrate on the rest of the service.

Nobody felt like having a big Sunday dinner, so they just snacked on cold cuts. Then Leona went to bed for a long nap. The children kept themselves busy quietly for a change. Fred tried to watch the football game on television. But when half-time came, he realized that he neither knew nor cared what the score was. He called Pastor Martin on the phone.

When the pastor answered, Fred said, "Hello, Pastor. It's Fred."

"How are you?" asked the pastor seriously.

"OK," said Fred, but he continued, "Pastor, I'm sorry to bother you on Sunday afternoon, but could you come over here and talk for a while?"

"Sure," said Pastor Martin. "I'll be right over." He got into his car and drove over to Fred's home. Being human, he was just a little bit annoyed that he would miss the second half of the football game. But being a pastor, he knew that it was his duty to be with someone who needed the comfort of God's word. He was also genuinely concerned about the spiritual welfare of his parishioners.

Fred ushered the pastor into the living room. He got them each a cup of coffee and then sat down and sighed. "Life is rough," he said.

"I know," the pastor replied.

"It was hard to listen to the Gospel lesson," Fred said. "The wife was quite upset about it."

"How did you take it?" Pastor Martin asked.

"Well," said Fred, "it was pretty bleak."

"I know," said Pastor Martin. "I thought about changing it because of what happened to your boy. A lot of other people in the congregation are mourning along with you."

"Why didn't you change it?" Fred asked.

The pastor responded, "I didn't change it from the traditional lesson because I figured that we should not run away from something in God's Word that might seem unpleasant. We can and should learn from everything in the Bible. But in the sermon I tried to answer the question that might be raised about the Gospel lesson."

Fred admitted, "I guess I didn't listen to the sermon too closely. My mind sort of wanders a lot lately."

After a pause, Fred asked, "But, Pastor, what about all those kids at Bethlehem that were killed? How many children must there have been? And God let them all get killed!"

The pastor said, "Bethlehem was a small town. I've read different estimates about how many children were killed. It may have been a dozen or so. It may have been more. But the number doesn't change anything. It was a very evil thing. It was an atrocity."

"Why did God let that happen? Doesn't God love children?" asked Fred.

"God loves everybody," replied the pastor. "But He is also wise. He is all-wise. Your children cannot understand how much wiser you are than they are. God is infinitely wiser yet. We cannot comprehend how much wiser he is than we are. We cannot understand his wisdom, and that is why we cannot understand his love. What he does and what he permits is all according to his wisdom, his justice, and his love."

Fred interrupted, "But how could it have been loving on God's part to let Herod kill all those children? How could it have been loving on God's part to let that hit-and-run driver kill my little boy?"

Pastor Martin responded, "We don't know, because we don't know what would have happened to those children if they had grown up. The children at Bethlehem were Christians like other Old Testament believers. They went to heaven. Your little boy was a Christian by virtue of his baptism. He is also in heaven now.

"Your wife cried when I read a passage that Matthew quoted from Jeremiah. Let me read you that verse from Jeremiah with the two following it: 'Thus saith the Lord: A voice was heard in Ramah, lamentation, and bitter weeping; Rahel weeping for her children refused to be comforted for her children, because they were not. Thus saith the Lord; Refrain thy voice from weeping, and thine eyes from tears; for thy work shall be rewarded, saith the Lord; and they shall come again from the land of the enemy. And there is hope in thine end, saith the Lord, that thy children shall come again to their own border' (Jeremiah 31:15-17). The Old Testament prophesied not just that the children would be killed but that they would go to heaven. Your boy has gone to heaven, even before you, his parents."

Fred protested, "But it doesn't seem fair for Jesus to be saved and all those others to get killed instead. The only reason they were killed was because Herod was out to get Jesus. And Jesus grew up — but those baby boys at Bethlehem did not grow up, and my son will not grow up."

The pastor answered, "Think about what you just said, Fred. You said that Jesus was saved but the other children got killed instead. That's what it looks like on the surface, but it is really the other way around."

"What do you mean?" Fred asked.

The pastor went on, "Jesus was saved from Herod only so that he could suffer under Pontius Pilate. Jesus did not die at Bethlehem only so that he could die at Jerusalem. Jesus did not die as a young child only so that he could die as a young man."

"You know, that's right." said Fred. "Jesus did not escape suffering by going to Egypt. He lived longer and suffered more."

"Yes," said the pastor. "And His suffering and death on the cross was in the place of those children from Bethlehem, and in your son's place, and in your place. He suffered and died so that we could live forever with him and his Father and his Spirit in the joy of heaven."

Fred said, "So whether a person lives one year or one hundred years isn't that important as long as he spends eternity with Christ."

"That's true," said Pastor Martin. "Or at least we can be content to leave it up to God how long someone lives — and what kinds of trials and temptations he permits for each of his Christians."

"I believe what you're saying, Pastor," said Fred, "but it still hurts. I'm still suffering, mourning."

"Yes," said the pastor, "I know. The pain and the sorrow are real. But we do have God's word, God's promise that the sufferings of this life will end, and that they are not worth comparing to the joy and glory that will be ours. Our trouble in this life is real. But none of us has to suffer as much as Jesus suffered for us. His suffering is what makes the difference."

"I believe what you're saying," said Fred. "It helps. I know that God will help me face the future. But why do Christians have to go through this pain?"

"Some go through more and some go through less," said Pastor Martin. "God sees to it that no Christian is overburdened. But the present world is very evil. God is showing mercy to us when we lose this world and everything in it. Even the people who seem to have everything lose it all when they die. God wants our thoughts and our hopes to be directed toward Him. Even our fondest hopes for our loved ones can be fulfilled only by God — and not in this life, either."

Fred told Leona and the children what the pastor had said. They were still just as sad about the death of their son and brother, but they had hope in the midst of their sorrow. They were sad the next time the holidays came and the youngest one in the family was not there to celebrate with them. But they looked forward to the time when the whole family would again be together to celebrate an unending holiday in the glory of heaven.

3 The Man Who Worried About Not Being Jewish

Read Matthew 8:5-13.

Fred got to be very active in his congregation. He went to Sunday services regularly, and he also read his Bible at home with his family. He went to a Bible class that the congregation offered. He was learning a lot, but he knew that he had a lot more to learn. He began to get bolder about telling others what he had learned from God's word.

Before this time Fred's co-workers had not even realized that Fred had any church connections at all. Fred began to tell them, as the opportunity arose, about the Lord Jesus. Some of them laughed at him, but they did not all laugh. Fred began to develop a friendship with a co-worker named Sam, who did not laugh when he heard Fred talk about Jesus. Sam was also very much involved in a local congregation that fitted into the general category called Fundamentalist.

Sam confessed faith in Christ. Fred believed that Sam was a genuine Christian, but he noticed that Sam had some strange ideas that did not square with the Bible. Fred was worried that these other ideas might lead Sam away from the central truth of forgiveness and salvation by Christ alone. Fred shared this concern with Sam. They talked about their different beliefs, but they did so without getting angry at one another.

One day Fred and Sam were eating lunch together. Sam brought up a topic that they had discussed before. He said, "Fred, I know we disagree about this, but I think it's important. Our minister preached about it again last Sunday. He said that God has never done away with his covenant with the Jews. He said that being born a physical descendant of Abraham gives a person a special claim on the kingdom of God.

"He said that all the Jews are going to be converted before Jesus comes again. They are going to keep their old laws. Then Jesus is going to set up his kingdom in Jerusalem and rule the earth for a thousand years. And the Jews are going to have a special place in that kingdom, all living in the Holy Land."

"Does your minister try to prove that from the Bible?" asked Fred.

"Sure. He quotes lots of Bible passages."

"Which ones?"

"He takes different passages from all over the Bible, you know, Ezekiel, and Daniel, and Revelation. Oh, lots from Revelation. It sure makes sense when he talks about it."

"Well," Fred said, I asked my pastor about it. He says that it does not make any difference whether one is born a Jew or a Gentile. Some Jews and some Gentiles are saved by God's grace in Christ. And some of both are damned, too. He showed me several places where the New Testament says that those who believe in Jesus are the people of God, no matter what they were born."

Sam objected, "But our minister goes to great lengths to prove that God will see to it that all the Jews get into his kingdom because they are still his chosen people. Gentiles have a harder time."

Fred asked, "How does he say that Gentiles can get into God's kingdom."

Sam went on, "He says that Gentiles do not have to keep all the old Jewish laws, but they do have to keep a lot of laws. We have to repent and give up all our old sins and just work at it until we get to the point where we don't sin anymore. Then we'll be good enough to get in. Believing in Jesus is important, but we also have to do lots of good works and stop sinning."

Fred asked, "Do you think you're going to make it that way?"

"I hope so, but I don't know."

"Are you sure you understand your minister and what he's saying?"

"I sure think so."

Then they noticed by the clock on the wall that it was time to get back to work. But Sam was worried about this disagreement. Sam was a bachelor, and he knew that Fred's wife Leona had taken the children to visit her parents for a few days. So he suggested that they meet in a certain restaurant for dinner that evening. Fred agreed, and they went back to work.

After work, on the way home to wash up and change clothes, Fred stopped to see Pastor Martin. He quickly outlined his conversation with Sam. Then he said, "Pastor, I need some help. Sam and I are getting together later to talk about this some more. Now you showed me several different places where the Bible talks about it pretty clearly, so I've got this straight in my own mind. But can you show me a simple way that I can clear it up for Sam?"

Pastor Martin said, "Fred, you're right. The best thing would be to keep attention focused on just one section from the Bible that is clear. That way you won't be misled, and maybe you can make the meaning clear to Sam. But remember that only the Holy Spirit can convince people of the truth."

The pastor thought for a few moments. Then he opened his Bible and laid it on the desk. Together he and Fred looked at Matthew 8:5-13, the story of the centurion from Capernaum. They talked about this passage for a while and about the approach Fred might use with Sam. Then Pastor Martin wrote down a couple of other verses Fred might use if he thought they would help. Fred left with some confidence that he knew what to say to Sam. But he was still a little worried.

When they met for dinner, Sam was carrying a huge Bible in a fancy leather case. It had at least eight hundred pages of Bible study helps. Involuntarily, Fred's hand felt for his pocket New Testament so that he did not feel totally unarmed, so to speak. During dinner they talked about news, sports, and weather. But over dessert Sam put his Bible up on the table and pulled out a large sheet of paper that his minister had given him. It was covered with references to the Bible, one verse from here and one verse from there, just skipping back and forth.

After they had looked at a few verses, Fred said, "Wait a minute! Let's not go on to the next verse so fast. Let's read the whole section where you got that last verse." When they did so, they found out that the verse was talking about something totally different from what it looked like when it was read out of context. Sam was a bit confused at that point.

Fred suggested, "Let's look at one section from the Bible which I think you will find interesting." Then he turned to Matthew 8:5-13, which they read together. Fred said, "Here is a story of a Gentile who believed in Jesus. Jesus did not tell him to get lost, or to get circumcised and become a Jew, or to do anything.

"And Jesus said that many Gentiles would come from the east and the west, from all over the world, and they would be saved. They would be with Abraham and Isaac and Jacob in the kingdom of heaven. And the kingdom of God is not some geographic location on this earth, for Jesus said, 'My kingdom is not of this world' (John 18:36). Some Jews and some Gentiles will be in that kingdom, and some of both will be out of it. Jesus says, too, that the sons of the kingdom would be cast into outer darkness."

"You're right," Sam had to admit. "There it is as plain as day. Where did I get steered wrong? What did this Gentile do to deserve to get into heaven, and what did some Jews do that they don't get in?"

Fred said, "You know, I've been thinking a lot about our conversation at noon. We ran out of time just after you told me how good you had to be to get into God's kingdom. And I asked you if you thought you were going to make it."

"Yes," said Sam, "and I've been worrying about it ever since."

Fred said gently, "I'm sorry you worried so long. I could have told you something from the Bible to take that worry away."

"What's that?"

"I wasn't thinking about this specific passage before, but it's in there, too. Look at the centurion. What does he say?"

Together they read the centurion's words, "Lord, I am not worthy that thou shouldest come under my roof."

Fred asked, "Did the centurion think he was good enough to deserve anything good from God?"

"No. No, he didn't," Sam replied.

Fred agreed, "That's right. He was not good enough. Neither are you and I. We are all sinners who have deserved from God only to be punished. I'm not judging you personally. That's what the Bible says about you and me."

Sam asked, "Then how can we hope to get to heaven?"

Fred went on, "That's the same as asking why this centurion hoped that Jesus would heal his servant. Why should God do anything good for us, and especially why should he take us to heaven? What did the centurion say?"

Together they read the centurion's next words: "But speak the word only, and my servant shall be healed. For I am a man under authority, having soldiers under me: and I say to this man, Go, and he goeth; and to another, Come, and he cometh; and to my servant, Do this, and he doeth it."

Sam said, "He pointed to Jesus' power."

"Right," said Fred. "He confessed that Jesus is all powerful and has all authority. He admitted that he was helpless. Only God could help. He confessed that Jesus is God as well as man. He trusted that Jesus' attitude toward him was favorable in spite of his sins. He believed that Jesus had come to die for the sins of the whole world. Maybe he had learned that from Jesus' own preaching or from that of John the Baptist. He believed that his sins were forgiven, and his faith was not disappointed. Jesus did die for his sins and for yours and mine. God is gracious to us because of Jesus' sacrifice."

Then Sam asked, "So it is only the centurion's faith that deserved salvation?"

Fred answered, "No. It doesn't say that the centurion deserved to be saved in any way. Faith does not deserve salvation. If it did, then salvation would not be the free gift the Bible says it is.

"The centurion believed in Jesus and in Jesus' word. Jesus' word is powerful. It was powerful to heal the servant at any distance. It is still powerful today. It was through God's word, by God's power, that the centurion had been brought to faith in Christ.

"We have read and shared the same word this evening. Through it God produces the faith that sins are forgiven and that God is gracious only for Jesus' sake."

Sam said suddenly, "The centurion trusted Jesus, not himself!"

"Right!"

"Then there is no different way for Jews than for Gentiles?"

"That's right. There is only one way for Jews and Gentiles. That way is the grace of God in Christ."

18

4. The Man Who Worried About Offerings

Read Luke 18:31-34.

One day Fred was eating lunch with some of his co-workers. His friend Sam was among them. Sam was taking the adult confirmation class to become a member of the congregation to which Fred belonged. But neither Fred nor Sam started talking.

One of the other fellows was dominating the conversation. He was griping about inflation. He was unhappy about the price of gasoline. He was upset that the utilities were going up. He was positively livid because the high interest rate had made it almost impossible for him to buy the new car that he had convinced himself he needed.

This man was no church-goer. He turned to Fred and Sam and said, "Everybody's getting ripped off these days. But you guys who give money to church are the biggest patsies of all. Don't you know that the preacher tells you to give money to the church just so he doesn't have to go out and get an honest job?"

Sam objected, "There may be some preachers like that, but not all of them. I used to go to a church where the preacher would check the offering plates. If he didn't think they were full enough, he'd send them around again. But it's different at the church I go to now."

The other man sneered, "I still say it's silly to give away any money at all, especially when everything is costing more all the time."

Fred did not take part in the conversation, but he listened to it closely. He thought about it much of the rest of the day. That evening after dinner, Fred and Leona were having an extra cup of coffee. The children had gone their separate ways, so the parents were alone.

Leona was telling Fred about her shopping trip that day. She said, "You wouldn't believe the prices!"

Fred was not listening too closely because he figured that this was a rerun. Then he realized that he really should listen to Leona because she was his wife. Besides, she might ask questions later. But he was saved by the bell, namely the doorbell.

It was one of the elders of the congregation, the elder in charge of stewardship. Fred took the visitor's coat and ushered him into the living room. Leona went to put on some more coffee.

Once they were all seated comfortably in the living room, the elder informed them that he had come on business. He explained, "You see, I want to talk to you about your offerings to the church. Now, we haven't singled you out. A group of us are making calls on all or most of the members to talk about the congregation's finances."

Fred observed, "Everybody's talking about money problems these days, what with inflation and all."

The elder responded, "That's right. But did you know that inflation really hits the church hard? Everything that the church has to buy costs more, too. According to the Bible, God wants us to pay the pastor a living wage for him and his family. Meanwhile many members are giving the same amount they gave years ago, even though their incomes have grown."

Fred asked, "So how much do you think we should give?"

The elder said, "That's for you to decide. I don't know how much you make, and I'm not asking. St. Paul once raised some money, but he did not make a command about how much or what percentage anyone should give. He wasn't forcing anyone to pay. He was asking them to give.

"He said, 'Every man according as he purposeth in his heart, so let him give; not grudgingly, or of necessity: for God loveth a cheerful giver' (2 Corinthians 9:7). And Paul didn't promise any great rewards for giving. But he did say — and remember, this is God's word — that God would see to it that Christians wouldn't suffer any shortage because of their generosity."

Fred suggested, "Then we should give only as much as we want to give."

The elder agreed, "That's right! The congregation doesn't send out bills. It's all a freewill offering. That's the only way the church receives money, when it's freely given. Paul tried to motivate people to give money, but he didn't do it by telling them they had to give. He did it by pointing out how much Jesus gave for us. He said, 'For ye know the grace of our Lord Jesus Christ, that, though he was rich, yet for your sakes he became poor, that ye through his poverty might be rich' " (2 Corinthians 8:9).

The whole conversation was very pleasant in tone, with no pressure, no hard-sell. The talk turned to other matters, and they each drank a couple cups of coffee while they talked. After the elder left, Fred and Leona were both thoughtful.

When Leona went to herd the younger children off to bed, Fred pulled his Bible off the shelf. He was thinking about something he had heard in church the previous Sunday, but he could not find it by thumbing through his Bible. Finally he had to go and hunt up the bulletin to find out what the sermon text had been. He looked it up and read it over.

When Leona came back, he said, "Honey, I've been thinking about last Sunday's sermon text."

Leona said, "I've forgotten what it was."

Fred read to her Luke 18:31-34. There Jesus told the apostles that he was going to be arrested, ridiculed, abused, tortured, and killed — and that he would rise from the dead on the third day, but the apostles did not understand what Jesus was saying.

Leona commented, "It's not too many months ago that those words didn't mean anything more to us than they meant to those disciples. Now they mean everything."

Fred said, "Ain't it the truth? Pastor Martin said Sunday that this text really tells us a lot about Jesus. Jesus knew that the Old Testament was God's word, that it had to be fulfilled. That's why Jesus came to earth, to fulfill what had been promised. That's why he became a man, and what a man he was, and is!"

Fred was deeply moved. He continued, "Yes. Jesus is quite a man. Imagine living all those years knowing what he was going to have to go through, knowing that he was going to the cross! He had to be really brave to head for Jerusalem!"

Leona picked up the thought, "He really loves us. Otherwise he wouldn't have done it."

Fred went on, "He didn't just give something. He gave everything."

"For us," Leona completed the thought.

Fred said, "He said He was going to die and rise again. If anyone else said that, he would be laughed at. Who can rise from the dead? But Jesus wasn't boasting. He said he was going to do it and he did it. He did it to earn the forgiveness of sins and eternal life and salvation for us. He suffered and died and rose again in our place."

Leona said, "When you think about what he had to go through, it kind of makes you ashamed to gripe about the hard times we have."

"Like I said," Fred repeated, "he didn't just give something. He gave everything.

Leona asked, "How much do you think we should give, Fred?"

Fred said, "Well, according to what he heard tonight, the Bible doesn't command a specific amount. But in the Old Testament, didn't they have to give ten percent?"

"Can we afford to give that much?" asked Leona.

Fred said, "Well, I'm going to take a look at our budget figures. Ten percent might not be a rule, but it looks like a good example to follow. Let's see if we can't take a stab at it."

"OK" said Leona, "let's talk about it. But remember that God also wants us to provide for the children."

"I know," said Fred. "We have to make responsible decisions. But now we know better what we should base the decisions on."

"That's right," said Leona brightening. "Besides, God has given us other things, too, like time itself. We should use time to serve the Lord."

"Leona, we really need to look at our whole lives in this way."

5. The Man Who Worried About His Neighbors

Read John 8:46-59.

It was a nice, sunny Saturday afternoon, the first really warm day of spring. Fred was outside raking his lawn and trying to decide whether he might get away without putting any fertilizer on this year. While Fred was lost in thought, his neighbor Dick came outside and called to him, "Hey, Fred, how ya doin'?"

Fred answered, "Oh, pretty good. Just trying to decide about the lawn here."

Dick came over and leaned on the fence. They joked about how they had better get their yardwork well under way before the summer sports season would start "when no man can work." They talked about various plans for the summer.

Dick almost complained about summer. He said, "You know, summertime is almost too busy. There's camping and boating and baseball and soccer. It's almost too much. Say, are you going to be part of our foursome again this summer, you know, to play golf on Sunday mornings?"

Fred hemmed and hawed, and then he came out with it, "No, Dick. I can't. The family and I are going to church regularly this summer. Golf got me away from church before, and it's not going to happen again."

Dick said, "Aw, it's too hot in summer to go to sit in a stuffy church and listen to a stuffy preacher give a stuffy sermon."

"If it's too hot in church," Fred replied, "it's too hot on the golf course. And we don't go to hear the preacher. We go to hear the word of God. Besides," Fred gulped and then continued, "besides, you and your family could use a little churchgoing yourselves."

Dick replied, "Don't give me that. We don't need church. We're pretty good people. The wife and I set a good example for the kids, and we try to teach them the Ten Commandments, you know, not to hit anybody unless he hits you first, and not to get pregnant before getting married. After all, that's what the Bible and church are all about."

"Well," Fred responded, "I think you may have missed the meaning of the Ten Commandments there. They say a lot more than that, and they are a lot tougher than you make them out to be."

"Get off my back. Nobody's perfect," Dick countered, "So what?"

"So God hates sin and he won't just forget about it," Fred replied. "There is forgiveness only for Jesus' sake. That's why we go to church, not just to hear about the Ten Commandments but especially to hear about Jesus. The Ten Commandments tell us that we aren't perfect, that we're a long way off from being perfect. And we need the forgiveness of sins. That's what we go to hear about."

Dick scoffed, "Oh, that Jesus was just another preacher way back when. I read about it in the newspaper. The newspaper said that Jesus just went around trying to teach people to love each other, and then some guys came along later and claimed that Jesus was God himself."

"Jesus was God, and Jesus is God," Fred stated. "He said so himself. And you need to know about him because he is your only hope of salvation."

"I'm doing all right," Dick replied. "I don't need your Jesus. And even if he himself claimed to be God, I wouldn't believe it. That would just make him another fake like all the rest."

Fred did not push it at that point. He wondered, though, what he could have said that would have made a difference to Dick. And he felt a bit guilty for not having convinced Dick. He still tried to be friendly with him, and they chatted a bit. Then they each went about their own business.

The rest of the day Fred was nagged by the thought that he should have said something different or something more. Leona told him not to worry about it. He had done his best to tell Dick about Jesus. He had tried to plant a seed. Let God worry about whether or not it was going to grow.

The next day was Sunday. Fred and Leona took the children to Sunday school, and then they went to Bible class. They were studying the eighth chapter of John's Gospel. Fred listened closely, but he did not participate very much. John 8 is a long chapter, but Pastor Martin led them through it all. He showed them the drama of Jesus' conflict with the Jews at Jerusalem in that chapter.

He showed them how Jesus claimed to be true God as well as true man, how Jesus described his relationship to God the Father, that they were one God but two different persons, two of the three persons of the Trinity.

Jesus said that those who did not believe he was true God would die in their sins. If someone did not believe in Jesus as God, he did not believe in Jesus at all. Our sins were very serious, and the death of a mere human being would not be sufficient to pay for the guilt of the whole world. Only the death of this person, who is both true God and true man, could pay for our sins.

Then they got to the last part of the chapter. Jesus challenged his enemies to show one sin that he had ever committed. No one could do it. Jesus asked them why they did not believe in him. Then he went on to tell them again about salvation through his word, and he emphasized again that he is true God, saying, "Before Abraham was, I am." Then the Jews tried to kill Him, but he got away miraculously.

Fred was thinking about the Bible study, but he was also thinking about Dick. He hesitated to compare his attempt to tell Dick about Christ with Christ's own preaching and speaking. But he finally asked Pastor Martin, "Why doesn't it always work when we tell people about Jesus? I mean, not everybody believed Jesus when He spoke, and certainly not everybody is going to believe us. Just yesterday . . . well, I don't know if you want to hear about what happened to me."

Pastor Martin said, "Sure, tell us, Fred. Maybe we can all learn something from it."

So Fred told them about his conversation with Dick. He did not want to brag about his efforts, but he genuinely wanted to learn something from the experience. So he told the story as accurately as he could remember it.

He concluded, "I was going to ask you, Pastor, what I had done wrong, but now I'm not sure that that would be the right question. Here today we learned that not everybody believed what Jesus had to say. We certainly can't suggest that he made any mistakes. But don't we also say that the Gospel is God's word, and that it has his power working through it?"

Pastor Martin answered, "Yes, we do, Fred. St. Paul says, 'I am not ashamed of the Gospel of Christ: for it is the power of God unto salvation to every one that believeth' (Romans 1:16). I would say that you did a fine job talking to your neighbor about Jesus.

"If he had believed, or if he had at least been interested enough to want to hear more, you would have to be careful not to get the idea that you could take any credit for it or

27

that he could take any credit. God deserves all the credit for bringing people to faith."

Fred said, "I understand that. But why doesn't it work?"

Pastor Martin answered, "It does work. It just doesn't work every time. Some people are brought to faith when they hear the word of God, and we give God the credit for that, just as the Bible does. But some people refuse to believe, and we blame them for that, just as the Bible does."

"So there is no explanation for why I believe but Dick doesn't even listen," Fred concluded.

"That's right," Pastor Martin agreed. "There is no explanation. There is only this fact, as Jesus pointed out in John 8. He told those who did not believe in him, 'He that is of God heareth God's words: ye therefore hear them not, because ye are not of God.' "

"Well, what can we do to make them listen?" Fred wondered.

Pastor Martin said, "We can only do what Jesus did. He continued to tell these unbelievers about himself, about who he is, about what he came to do for them and for the whole world. Jesus talked about himself and his work. We can only keep talking to people about Jesus and about how he died on the cross for their sins, too."

Fred asked, "Then I shouldn't give up on Dick, should I?"

Pastor Martin answered, "No. You should talk to him about Jesus again when you have the opportunity. But if he gets too angry about it, you might as well pull back and wait for another opportunity. Meanwhile you could tell someone else about Jesus. After all, Dick isn't the only unbeliever you know."

Sunday afternoon Fred was out raking the lawn again. He was not the fastest raker in the world. In fact, he was beginning to wonder how best to suggest to one of his boys that the Fourth Commandment just might include helping dear old dad with the yardwork.

Fred was raking on the side of his yard where his neighbor Tony lived. Tony came out of the house and called to him, "Hey, Fred, how ya doin'?"

28

Fred answered, "Oh, pretty good."

Tony came over and leaned on the fence. He said, "I hear you're not going to be playing golf with us on Sunday mornings this year."

"That's right," said Fred. "Golf got me away from church in the past, and it's not going to happen again. Church is too important to me and my family."

Tony said, "But isn't it too hot in summer to go and sit in a stuffy church and listen to a stuffy preacher give you a stuffy sermon?"

"No, it's not too hot," Fred insisted. "And besides, we don't go to hear the preacher. We go to hear the word of God."

Tony said, "But you can read the Bible at home, can't you?"

Fred told him, "We do read the Bible at home, but we found out that when we stopped going to church, we stopped reading the Bible at home, too. And it's God's will that we get together with our fellow Christians to hear his word proclaimed publicly."

Tony asked, "Doesn't that preacher just tell you a big list of do's and don't's? Who needs that? Nobody's perfect. So what?"

"So God hates sin and he won't just forget about it," Fred replied. "There is forgiveness only for Jesus' sake. That's really why we go to church, not because of the church but because of Jesus Christ. God's law tells us that we aren't perfect, that we aren't even within waving distance of keeping his commandments. And we need the forgiveness of sins. That's what we go to hear about."

"Who was Jesus, anyway?" Tony asked. "Son of God? What does that mean?"

"Jesus was — and is — true God, God the Son, who was also born a man," Fred explained. "He lived a perfect life but was punished for everybody else's sins — your sins, too."

"I don't know," Tony commented.

"You should hear more," Fred suggested.

"Maybe I should," Tony admitted.

6. The Man Who Worried About Waiting

Read John 16:16-23.

Fred had a co-worker named Sam. Through conversations with Fred, Sam had become involved in the same congregation and was taking adult confirmation instruction. Fred and Sam were not only friends and co-workers. They also became fishing buddies.

Early one Saturday morning in spring, Fred got up long before the sun, quietly fixed his own breakfast, and got his fishing tackle ready. Sam came by to pick him up, and they drove up to the lake.

Once there, they got into Sam's little boat and rowed over to a likely looking spot to wet a line. After baiting their hooks, they cast them out and settled down to wait for a nibble. At first they were very quiet as fishermen should be. But as they got a little bit bored with waiting, they began to converse in low tones, hoping not to scare the fish away.

It seems that Sam had a few problems and wanted to talk to Fred about them. He said, "Uh, Fred, things haven't been going too well lately."

"How so?" asked Fred.

"Oh," said Sam, "a lot of little things, and a few big ones. There are problems at work, but you already know about them. Then my girl friend broke up with me since I stopped going to that Fundamentalist church I used to attend with her. And I've been having some trouble with my health. The doctor says I may need an operation."

Fred could not think of anything to say except, "Everybody has problems like that sometimes."

Sam went on, "Now my folks tell me that all these problems show that I'm not a good enough Christian. They say that if I believed hard enough and lived a better life, why, then all my problems would disappear."

"Do you believe that?" asked Fred.

Sam said, "I used to. I used to hear that all the time in church, you know, that we had to do something to make God happy with us. But I'm hearing something different in our congregation. I'm hearing just as much about how I'm a sinner and all that. In fact, more so. I'm learning that I'm such a sinner that I can't save myself or even help myself at all. But I also hear that God isn't mad at me, that my sins are forgiven for Jesus' sake. I hear that God himself gives me the faith to receive this forgiveness. Then I hear that God also makes all my problems work together for my good and blessing, that God's love and grace and goodness will never fail me. But sometimes it's confusing."

"I think you should talk to Pastor Martin about this," Fred suggested. "A pastor needs to hear about these things if he is going to help you with your trouble."

Sam assured Fred, "I will discuss them with the pastor, but he's not here now. What do you think, Fred?"

Fred told him, "I have an uncle, my Uncle Fritz. He got to listening to this preacher on television who kept on promising miracles if you'd only believe hard enough and do some good works, like sending money to support his TV show. Uncle Fritz had his share of problems, too. His wife was very sick, and one of his kids was getting divorced. Uncle

Fritz started believing this preacher, sending money, and the whole bit."

"What happened?" asked Sam.

"Nothing," said Fred. "None of his problems got solved that way. Poor old Uncle Fritz just got taken to the cleaners."

"Fleeced, eh?" said Sam.

"Yep," said Fred. "Now my uncle hardly goes to church at all, all because of some television preacher who made a bunch of promises he couldn't deliver on."

Sam asked, "So what does that all mean? My question still hasn't been answered. Why doesn't God just solve all our problems right away?"

Fred sat up straight, stretched his shoulders, and shifted his position in the boat in order to be more comfortable. Then he said, "That's just like asking why we have to wait so long to catch a fish."

"In a way, it is," Sam agreed.

Then Fred told Sam a story, "You remember how our youngest boy was killed by a hit-and-run driver on New Year's Eve?"

Sam said, "Yeah. You told me about it, about how you were pretty broken up at the time."

"Well," said Fred, "the other day I saw Leona sitting at the dining room table crying. I asked her what was wrong. She told me that with spring she was seeing so many children playing outside and she really missed the boy."

"What did you say to her?"

"I just felt helpless. I didn't have any answers. So we went to see Pastor Martin. He reminded us about Easter. Jesus' resurrection means that our boy and all the dead in Christ will be raised again. Actually, everybody who has ever died will be raised, but the unbelievers will be raised only to be punished. But all who believe and are baptized like our boy was will be raised to everlasting life.

"Well, Leona still felt sad because it might be a long time before we're all together in heaven or before the last day when we're all raised together. But then Pastor Martin said that when that time comes, we won't even remember the sorrow and the waiting because we'll be so happy to be reunited. It really helped to hear that."

Sam chimed in, "You know, this may sound strange, but I had some interesting thoughts on the Saturday before Easter. On Good Friday we all heard in church about Jesus' death on the cross for the forgiveness of our sins. And we knew that on Easter Sunday we were going to hear about Jesus' resurrection. So on the Saturday in between I wasn't really sad. It was a good time to think. I was thinking about how the disciples must have felt between Jesus' death and resurrection. They didn't know that Jesus was going to rise from the dead."

Fred pulled his New Testament out of his tackle box and thumbed through it. He said, "Here's what Pastor Martin showed us. After supper on Maundy Thursday, Jesus told his disciples, 'A little while, and ye shall not see me: and again, a little while, and ye shall see me.' Then a few verses later, Jesus said, 'Verily, verily, I say unto you, That ye shall weep and lament, but the world shall rejoice: and ye shall be sorrowful, but your sorrow shall be turned into joy. A woman when she is in travail hath sorrow, because her hour is come: but as soon as she is delivered of the child, she remembereth no more the anguish, for joy that a man is born into the world. And ye now therefore have sorrow: but I will see you again, and your heart shall rejoice, and your joy no man taketh from you.' "

Sam said, "That's beautiful."

Fred responded, "Even more important, it's true. Those disciples had their 'little while' when they were sad, waiting and wondering and worrying. But it was just a little while for them. When they saw Jesus again, risen from the dead, the time they had been mourning must have meant nothing to them, they were so happy."

Sam picked up the thought, "It's just like Jesus said. Their sorrow was turned into joy. They had been really sad. But then they were happier than they had ever been before. They have that happiness now in heaven."

Fred continued, "And, you know, really that is the answer to all our questions and problems. The disciples knew about their sins, and they wanted God to be pleased with them in spite of their sins, to accept them anyway. When Jesus died on the cross, God's anger was satisfied, but the disciples didn't know it yet. They worried, I guess, whether they had been wrong about Jesus, whether Jesus might have been just another sinful human being."

Sam interrupted, "But when Jesus came back to life, then everything was clear for them. Then everything made sense to them. Is that what you're saying?"

Fred replied, "Exactly! Then they understood that Christ had to die on the cross to pay for their sins. They understood that he had died for the sins of the whole world, and they understood that his resurrection meant that God's anger against sin was appeased because God the Son died on the cross."

Sam said, "So the point is that none of my problems means that God has not forgiven my sins or that I have to do something yet to earn his love or favor."

"Right!" Fred agreed. "Jesus has already taken care of that. God sends us problems and troubles for various reasons, or at least he lets them happen to us. But they are never punishment for us. God wants to correct us or to get our attention, or just to show us that we cannot trust ourselves and must rely only on him."

Sam said, "God doesn't want to let us be sad, not for long, anyway, just for a little while."

"Even if that 'little while' seems pretty long to us," Fred replied, "it really is just a little while compared to everlasting life and the joy we will have with the Lord forever."

"And when the sadness is over, we won't wonder about it anymore," Sam added.

Fred responded, "Well, what the pastor said was that when we look back on this life from the next world, we will see God's purpose behind everything. We'll see that, for us believers, it was all for our spiritual good."

Suddenly Sam's bobber went under the water. Then Fred's went under, too. They jerked their poles at the same time to set the hooks. In the excitement of landing their fish they forgot the weariness and the boredom of waiting. When they had put them on the stringer, Sam exclaimed, "That was worth waiting for!"

7. The Man Who Worried About a Sinner

Read Luke 15:1-7.

One Sunday morning Fred arrived at church with his family and saw someone he had not seen there before. It was a man Fred had known from his schooldays. His name was Biff. Maybe that was his nickname, but it was the name by which most people knew him. He was a rough-and-tumble sort of guy. Fred learned later that someone from the congregation had simply invited him to come to church.

Fred did not listen to the sermon very closely that Sunday. He was reminiscing about his schooldays. He remembered Biff, all right. Biff had been something of a bully. He remembered how Biff had beaten him up when they were both in the ninth grade. His jaw had hurt for weeks.

One thought led to another. Fred remembered Biff from their time in high school. It was not that Fred had been close to Biff at all. It was that everybody knew about Biff! He had been quite the ladies' man. And there were rumors about him getting into trouble with the law.

Fred remembered more and more. He hardly noticed it, but he began to think: why should Biff be coming to church? He had never darkened a church door in his life! Imagine that! After living the kind of life he has been living all these years, he thinks he can just walk into church as pretty as you please and sit down with all the good church-goers! Fred even began to feel the pain in his jaw from when Biff had beaten him up.

Fred succeeded in avoiding Biff on the way out of church. But Biff kept coming to church, and it became harder and harder to avoid him. Then one evening the men of the congregation were going to have dinner in the banquet room of a local restaurant. Fred got there a little late. There was only one place left. Fred would have to sit next to Biff. He went and greeted Biff as politely as he could. They shook hands, and Fred remembered how strong Biff was.

They had barely finished their salads when Biff said, "I've been meaning to talk to you, Fred, but you always seem to rush out of church."

"Well, you know, uh, there's lots of things to do on Sunday," Fred tried to excuse himself. "Busy, busy! No rest for the wicked and all that."

Biff said. "Sure. I know. But I wanted to talk to you about," he lowered his voice, "about when we were kids. I know I beat you up once or twice."

Fred thought to himself, "Twice! I'd forgotten that! Why that no-good . . . "

Biff went on, "Yeah, well, I just wanted to apologize for it. I know it's been a few years. But I just wanted to say, 'No hard feelings,' eh?"

"Sure, no hard feelings. I'd forgotten all about it." They shook hands again.

Biff kept on talking, "Some really strange things have been happening to me lately. I really hit rock bottom. I knew I needed help. One of the guys from work invited me to church. I found out what my problem has been all these years. You know what it was?"

"No, what?"

"Sin! It was sin! Who'd've thought? I finally found out I was a sinner. Oh, I guess I sort of knew it all along. I just mean, hearing the pastor talk about sin, I finally admitted to myself and to God that I was a real hard-core sinner. Then I sure wanted God to forgive me. Now hearing about how God's Son died for my sins, too, that's music to my ears."

Fred noticed just a little tear in Biff's eye. They both ignored it — Fred, because he was embarrassed, Biff, because he was not.

Biff continued, "That's why I wanted to apologize to you, too. I want to get along with everybody in the church. I want to belong. You know, I'm taking the pastor's adult confirmation class. Pastor Martin has been really great, welcomed me right into the church and the class. I was afraid he wouldn't want somebody with my reputation in the church."

They talked about this and that through the rest of the meal. Then they shared the same Bible during the Bible study that followed. When the others started going home, Fred stayed behind. He wanted to talk to Pastor Martin.

Fred and Pastor Martin decided to sit and drink another cup of coffee while they talked. Pastor Martin asked, "Something wrong, Fred?"

Fred said, "Pastor, do you know what you're doing, letting that Biff take adult instruction? Why, he may become a communicant member of the congregation!"

"I certainly hope so," said Pastor Martin.

"But, but," said Fred, "you must not know about his reputation."

"I've heard," said the pastor, "but I've tried not to listen."

Fred said, "What I could tell you . . . "

Pastor Martin interrupted, "You could but you won't, right?"

"OK, OK," said Fred. "So gossip is a sin against the Eighth Commandment. But this could be called public knowledge. What will people think of our church if we accept people like that?"

"I hope," said Pastor Martin, "that they will know that our church preaches the forgiveness of sins for Jesus' sake."

Pastor Martin could see that Fred was not happy. He took a deep breath and said, "Listen, Fred. You should know that there is a big difference between forgiveness and approval. Look at Jesus. We know that he disapproves of sin. He preached the law very strictly. Nobody who reads the Bible could think that Jesus approves of sin. Jesus doesn't approve of sin, but he does forgive sin. There's a big difference.

"In fact, to forgive sin without approving of it is the reason God the Son became a man. He came to be guilty in God's eyes for all our sins, for all the sins of the whole human race. He came to suffer the full punishment so that we could be forgiven for all our sins. And we have been forgiven for that reason alone."

"But Biff . . . , " Fred protested.

Pastor Martin interrupted him, "But Biff is no different from you or me. He knows he's a sinner because his life doesn't measure up to the Ten Commandments. But neither does your life or mine. And Biff knows his sins are forgiven for Jesus' sake alone. And that is the only reason your sins and mine are forgiven. God doesn't accept us because we are good. We are not good. God accepts us because Jesus is good."

Fred was still upset, and Pastor Martin could see it quite clearly. He said, "Fred, something's still bugging you, and I'm not asking what it is unless you want to tell me."

After a pause, Pastor Martin went on, "Do you remember Jesus' parable about the shepherd who had a hundred sheep? I preached about it a few weeks ago, in fact, the first Sunday Biff was in church. This shepherd had a hundred sheep, and one got lost. The shepherd left the ninety-nine and went to look for that one. He looked until he found it, and then he carried it back on his shoulders. Jesus said that the shepherd was happier about the one that was lost and then found than about the ninety-nine that never got lost."

"So?" asked Fred.

"Who is that one sheep that was lost and then found?" Pastor Martin asked.

"I suppose you're going to tell me that's Biff," Fred replied.

"No," Pastor Martin said, "I'm going to tell you that it's you. It's you, and it's me, and it's Biff, and it's every Christian. There's no one in the world who hasn't gone astray. And there's no Christian who's a Christian for any other reason than this, that the Good Shepherd found him and brought him back. You know that Isaiah says, 'All we like sheep have gone astray; we have turned every one to his own way; and the Lord hath laid on him the iniquity of us all'" (Isaiah 53:6).

Listening to these words, Fred's expression changed and his attitude changed. He said, "You're right, Pastor. I've forgotten everything I ever knew about Christianity, I was so upset with Biff. But I remember how we learned in catechism class that Jesus has redeemed me, even though I was lost and condemned on my own. Pastor, I've been all wrong in my attitude toward Biff. I should have known better."

"Yes, you should have known better," Pastor Martin agreed, "but you know, the old Adam is still around. The old sinful nature still clings to us. Even the firmest Christians are in danger of slipping into that kind of attitude. Perhaps I should say that that is one temptation that hits the firmest Christians the hardest. It's the temptation to be proud."

"I'm really sorry," Fred confessed. "I'm really ashamed of myself."

Pastor Martin assured him, "Christ died for that sin, too. It is forgiven. Don't worry."

Because he believed in the forgiveness of sins, his own as well as Biff's, Fred began to think about Biff as a friend and more than a friend, as a brother in Christ. And he began to look for ways to treat Biff as a brother. Fred's attitude had been changed, but it was not Fred that had changed it. It was the word of God.

8. The Man Who Worried About the Law

Read Romans 6:23.

One day Fred came home from work very upset. He stormed into the house and slammed the door. As usual, the family was there to greet him. The first to get to Fred was their pet dog with his tail wagging. Fred ignored the pet, but dogs are not easily discouraged. He jumped up and put his paws on Fred's legs. Fred pushed him away and scolded, "Get down! Bad dog!"

Then Leona met him with a kiss. She said, "Hi, Honey! How was your day?" Then she noticed a large tear in his shirt and asked, "How did you tear your shirt?"

"What does it matter?" Fred asked nastily.

"Sorry. I was just asking," Leona apologized.

"Well, if you must know," Fred grumbled, "I tore it on the car door at the parking lot this morning. And everybody's been asking me about it all day."

Then their ten-year-old daughter came running up. She said, "Daddy, Daddy, look what I made at school today."

"Not now," Fred put her off.

She went on, "Daddy, how did you tear your shirt?"

Fred said angrily, "If one more person asks me that question, . . . "

The little girl looked very sad. Tears came to her eyes. That was enough to melt Fred's heart, even on a day like that. He knelt down and said, "I'm sorry, Princess. Look, Daddy's had a rough day. He's just tired, OK? You run along and play now. After dinner, we'll watch our favorite TV show together, OK?"

Fred was still not feeling very good. But he was able to control himself through the dinner hour. Then, before anybody went off to do anything else, they had their customary family devotions. Fred read from the Bible and from a devotional book. Then they said the Apostles' Creed and the Lord's Prayer together. Fred added another prayer.

Then they all went off somewhere, everyone but Fred. He still sat there looking at the Bible. He opened it again to the chapter he had read for devotions. It was bothering him because it said some pretty strict things about sin. Fred felt bad. He knew that he had been far from perfect. He knew that he still sinned a lot every day, in spite of all the churchgoing and Bible-reading he had been doing.

He decided to look for some comfort in the Bible. He came upon these verses: "Know ye not that the unrighteous shall not inherit the kingdom of God? Be not deceived: neither fornicators, nor idolaters, nor adulterers, nor effeminate, nor abusers of themselves with mankind, nor thieves, nor covetous, nor drunkards, nor revilers, nor extortioners, shall inherit the kingdom of God" (1 Corinthians 6:9,10).

That was not what Fred needed to hear. Instead of being comforted, he was more anxious than ever. He saw himself being condemned for his sins. He had not done all of those things, but he had done or had wanted to do some of them. He really began to worry.

He tried to think of some comforting Bible passages, but all he could think of was the law. He remembered that Jesus had said, "For I say unto you, That except your righteousness shall exceed the righteousness of the scribes and Pharisees, ye shall in no case enter into the kingdom of heaven" (Matthew 5:20). He remembered, "The wages of sin is death."

Leona came back into the dining room. She said, "Fred, it's time for that show. You promised the kids that you'd watch it with them."

Fred got up and went into the television room. He really did not want to watch television right then, but he always tried to keep his promises to the children.

Fred sat down in his favorite chair. The daughter he had scolded before came and sat in his lap. The children were happy to see their father take an interest in something they all enjoyed. Usually Fred liked this show. It was good, clean humor, unlike most of the junk on television. But tonight, Fred just could not get his mind off of God's law. He just could not enjoy the show.

The comic said, "Good evening, Ladies and Germs."

Fred thought, "The wages of sin is death."

The comic said, "Did you hear the one about the power line? No? It's over your head."

Fred thought, "The wages of sin is death."

The kids were laughing so loudly that they did not hear the next joke.

Fred thought, "The wages of sin is death."

After the show, Fred was supposed to help his son with his memory work for confirmation class. That did not help Fred at all. Every time he heard Dr. Luther's explanation of one of the Commandments in the *Small Catechism*, it condemned him. Every time he heard, "We should fear and love God," he knew that he had not feared and loved God as he should have.

The children went to bed. Leona went to bed. Still Fred sat up, trying to read, trying not to think about the wages of sin. When he finally did turn in, he had trouble getting to sleep. He was worried about his relationship to God. For he knew: "The wages of sin is death."

The next morning he told Leona that he was still both-ered about how nasty he had been when he had come home the previous evening. Leona said, "Forget it. It doesn't matter. Nobody's perfect."

"Yeah, but a Christian husband and father shouldn't be like that," Fred insisted.

"Look, Mr. Super-Christian," Leona replied, "you can't forget that you're still human. You had a rough day. That's all. It happens to everybody. Today will be better, right?" I mean, after yesterday, the only way to go is up. Cheer up. Otherwise the kids will think there's something wrong."

But that did not help Fred either. So he took time out at work to call Pastor Martin. He arranged to stop on his way home from work to see the pastor. Then he called Leona to tell her that he would be a bit late. He did not give her any further explanation.

When Pastor Martin had welcomed Fred into his study late that afternoon, they chatted a bit about this and that. Pastor Martin could see that Fred was uneasy, but he let Fred get around to serious matters in his own time. Finally Fred said, "Pastor, what I wanted to see you about, well, I'm worried about something I read in the Bible. I mean, I guess I just don't understand it."

"What's that?"

"It's where Jesus says, 'Except your righteousness shall exceed the righteousness of the scribes and Pharisees, ye shall in no case enter into the kingdom of heaven.' "

"What about it?" asked the pastor.

"Doesn't that say that we have to be saved by our own good works?" Fred asked.

"No," said the pastor, "not when you read the whole fifth chapter of Matthew in context. Jesus was telling the people that they would have to be absolutely perfect if they were going to save themselves by works. He was telling them that they could not be saved that way."

"But if that's true," Fred asked, "how can we be saved? You can't just ignore the fact that Jesus said that there's no way to get to heaven except by having more righteousness than the Pharisees."

Pastor Martin replied, "Fred, the same Jesus also said, 'Come unto me, all ye that labor and are heavy laden, and I will give you rest' (Matthew 11:28). He also said that He had come 'to give his life a ransom for many' (Matthew 20:28). He also told that criminal on the cross next to his, 'Today thou shalt be with me in paradise!" (Luke 23:43).

Fred opened the pastor's Bible and said, "But I also read this in the Bible: 'Know ye not that the unrighteous shall not inherit the kingdom of God?' (1 Corinthians 6:9). And then there is a long list of the sinners that won't get into heaven. I'm really disturbed. With these verses, how can we say that we are saved just because of what Jesus did? But if we have to do something, I haven't been good enough. I know that."

The pastor took the Bible and said, "But Fred, you stopped too soon. You didn't read the next verse after that list of sinners. That verse says, "And such were some of you: but ye are washed, but ye are sanctified, but ye are justified in the name of the Lord Jesus, and by the Spirit of our God' (1 Corinthians 6:11). So, you see, the Bible condemns sin and sinners — but it also forgives. Forgiveness is the key thing."

Fred said, "I don't know what's wrong, Pastor, but I just can't seem to get it out of my mind. There's one passage that just keeps going around and around, and I can't stop thinking about it."

"Which one is that?"

"The wages of sin is death."

"Do you know what comes next?"

"No, I don't. I was trying to remember and I couldn't. I couldn't remember where it is in the Bible, either."

The pastor handed the Bible back to Fred and said, "Look it up. It's Romans 6:23."

Fred flipped through the Bible until he found the passage. He read it silently. Then he read it aloud: "The wages of sin is death; but the gift of God is eternal life through Jesus Christ our Lord."

Fred looked at the pastor and said, "Even this one verse says both things."

"That's right, Fred," said the pastor. "The Bible tells us both things. It says that God demands perfect obedience. But it also says that God forgives our sins for Jesus' sake. He gives us eternal salvation as a free gift, without us doing anything to earn or deserve it."

Fred said, "This is what you're always talking about as 'law and gospel,' right?"

"You got it," Pastor Martin agreed.

Fred said, "But what I've gotta know is, which one is for me? If it's the law for me, then I'm going to hell. If it's the gospel for me, then I'm going to heaven. Which one is for me?"

"Both," said the pastor.

"How can that be?" asked Fred.

Pastor Martin said, "They are both for you, Fred, but for different purposes, and at different times. The law condemns your sin, and it will condemn your sin as long as you're a sinner; that will be as long as you're in this life. So anytime you read those passages, you are going to know that you were and are a sinner. That's what those passages are for, to tell you and to keep on telling you that you are a sinner.

"It doesn't mean that you are going to hell for sure, but it means that without Christ you would go to hell for sure. If you would read that whole section in Romans 6, you would see that's what it means. Without Christ, you would go to hell. But when you are made aware of your sinfulness, you should not stay with those passages. They will only lead you to despair. That's where you were at when you came in here today."

"What should I do?" asked Fred.

Pastor Martin told him, "You must learn to turn to the gospel when the law condemns your sins. I showed you how you would have come upon the gospel if only you had kept on and read further in the Bible."

Fred said, "I guess I don't know the Bible well enough."

"I don't know it well enough, either," the pastor admitted. "We all have to keep learning God's word all our lives. That's one good reason why it is important to keep on reading the Bible at home and coming to church and Bible class. But you don't have to be a great scholar or memorize the whole Bible to be able to turn from the law to the gospel. Why don't you just, right now, memorize that one verse, Romans 6:23: 'For the wages of sin is death; but the gift of God is eternal life through Jesus Christ our Lord.' "

Fred started repeating the verse: "For the wages of sin is death; but the gift of God is eternal life through Jesus Christ our Lord. For the wages of sin is death." That first part was easy to say but hard to hear. He found great joy and comfort in the second part: "But the gift of God is eternal life through Jesus Christ our Lord."

Fred kept on repeating that verse on the way home. When he got home, he was really happy. The dog came running up, wagging his tail. Fred stooped down to scratch him behind the ears and tell him he was a good dog. He had a big kiss for Leona. He took time to listen to everything the children wanted to tell him.

"See, I told you things would go better at work today," Leona reminded him.

Fred smiled and said, "It was a lousy day at work. It was even worse than yesterday. But I don't care."

Leona said suspiciously, "Where were you? Did you go and have one with the boys?"

"No," Fred said, "I'm really happy, but not for that reason. I'll tell you all about it — at family devotions."

9. ■ The Man Who Worried About the Flesh

Read Galatians 5:16-24.

Fred and Leona had a great deal of respect for the Bible. They knew that it was the word of God, and they knew that the Holy Spirit used it as his tool in their lives, to bring them all kinds of spiritual benefits. They wanted these same benefits for their children.

So they went to church and Bible class. They sent the children to Sunday school and confirmation class. They also used the Bible in their home. They each did their own personal Bible reading and encouraged the children to do the same. They also sat together after supper and read a chapter from the Bible aloud.

One week they had decided to go through St. Paul's Epistle to the Galatians. They started on Monday, and so they were reading the fifth chapter on Friday. As the father and head of the family, Fred recognized that God wanted him to be the pastor and bishop in his own home. So Fred took the lead in these family devotions.

But on this particular Friday evening he had trouble reading the fifth chapter of Galatians, especially the list of the works of the flesh. He stumbled at the end of the list when he read, "Of the which I tell you before, as I have also told you in time past, that they which do such things shall not inherit the kingdom of God."

Fred stumbled when he read that. It was unusual for him to stumble, for he was a good reader. But no one seemed to notice. Actually, one of the children was watching the dog. One of the children was thinking about plans for that evening, since it was Friday. Leona was a bit distracted because she had a cake in the oven and was watching the timer. So no one noticed that Fred was bothered when he read those verses.

Later, when they were alone, Fred mentioned this chapter again to Leona. He asked, "Honey, were you, uh, you know, bothered at all by our chapter from the Bible tonight?"

"No. Why?"

"Well, it was pretty strict about right and wrong."

"To tell you the truth, I guess I wasn't listening very closely."

"Yeah. That happens. But I was really upset."

"What do you mean?"

"Uh, well, I don't know if we need to go into it in detail."

"But now I'm curious. So why don't you tell me exactly what it is that's bothering you."

"OK. Let's look at it." He pulled out their Bible again and opened it to Galatians 5. "Look at this list of sins," he said.

Leona read it over and commented, "But you and I don't live like that."

Fred said, "Well, I haven't exactly done all those things. I mean, it mentions adultery. Now, you trust me. I've never committed adultery, but I can't exactly say I've never looked at another woman. And there's idolatry. I've never bowed down to a statue or prayed to the Virgin Mary. But God has not always come first in my thinking, and he doesn't always come first now, not all the time.

"And look at all these other things. All right, I haven't gotten drunk very often in my life. But there have been times. And we've had a pretty happy marriage, but we've quarreled a few times, too. And we don't always get along so smoothly with the kids. Need I go on?"

"No," said Leona, "you don't need to go on. But why is this bothering you right now?"

"Well," Fred said, "it's that verse there: 'They which do such things shall not inherit the kingdom of God.' "

"But Fred, you've worried about this before," Leona reminded him, and Pastor Martin told you to comfort yourself with the forgiveness of sins. Aren't you forgetting about forgiveness? That's what Jesus died on the cross for. The way you're talking, no one would ever get to heaven."

"Yeah," said Fred. "You're right. And I know you're right."

Just then one of the children came in and needed or wanted something. Fred's paternal instincts took over, and he forgot about his worries for the time being.

The next day was Saturday, and Fred did not have to work. He was out and about, running errands, and worrying in the back of his mind about the same Bible passages. He decided to run over to the church and talk to the pastor, hoping he would be there.

Fred found Pastor Martin sitting at the typewriter in his office. The pastor saw him and said, "Hi, Fred. Come on in and have a seat."

Fred told the pastor about reading Galatians 5 and about the conversation he had had with Leona.

When he was finished, Pastor Martin said, "Fred, it sounds to me like Leona was telling you what you needed to hear. The passage you were concerned about was a pretty strict statement of God's law. Leona was right to direct you to the gospel, the good news of the forgiveness of sins for Jesus' sake."

"But, Pastor," Fred protested, "I know we've talked about it all before. Still it seems like you're taking one thing the Bible says and playing it off against another thing."

Pastor Martin said, "In a way, I am, Fred. You remember we talked about this in Bible class. It's called the distinction between law and gospel. The law is 100% strict, and the gospel is 100% forgiving. From Mount Sinai you can't see Mount Calvary. But, from Mount Calvary you can't see Mount Sinai either.

Fred asked, "What do you mean?"

The pastor explained, "We were taught in seminary that we should preach the law as if there were no gospel. That is what you have in those verses you were reading — the law as if there were no gospel. But we were also taught to preach the gospel as if there were no law. That is found in many passages in the Bible. Biblical preaching means just that — preaching the law as if there were no gospel and the gospel as if there were no law."

"Nice words, Pastor," said Fred, "but doesn't this section of Galatians stand, too? Isn't that the word of God? We can't deny it, can we?"

"You've got a point, Fred," admitted the pastor. "It is the word of God. But it is not the whole word of God. It is God's law. But there is also the gospel. If you take just one part of the Bible and act as if that were the whole Bible, you're going to be missing an awful lot."

"It's beginning to make sense, I guess," Fred agreed. "If I could just be sure!"

Pastor Martin continued, "Jesus did not come on earth to tell us that we had to keep the law to go to heaven. He came to give his life as a ransom for us. That's what he himself said about it. If you had to live up to the law sections of the Bible to get to heaven, you wouldn't make it, and neither would I. Nobody would. Only Jesus never sinned."

"I know that," said Fred. "That's what I was worried about."

The pastor said, "Fred, I tell you that all your sins were laid on the spotless Lamb of God, who died on the cross for the forgiveness of all your sins and rose again to prove and certify that forgiveness."

"I believe that," Fred agreed. "The Bible says that, too."

"Sure it does," said the pastor.

"But what are we to make of these verses in Galatians 5?" Fred asked.

Pastor Martin said, "You missed the key to what they mean. You have to read it all in the light of verse 17: 'For the flesh lusteth against the Spirit, and the Spirit against the flesh: and these are contrary the one to the other; so that ye cannot do the things that ye would.' "

Fred was still puzzled and asked, "How does that clear it up?"

Pastor Martin went on, "The point here is that you don't have to be perfect to be saved. In fact, you can't be perfect, not in this life. Neither you nor any other Christian can live without sin. We still have that old Adam, the sinful flesh. The old sinful nature with its inherited tendency to sin is very strong. It's on the way out in Christians, but it is not gone, not yet, not in this life. It is still in us, struggling with the spiritual life that has been given to us and is growing."

"You know," said Fred, "we all had to take some kind of psychology test at work recently. The shrink told me that I was at war with myself, but he didn't have too much time to tell me what he meant. And I really considered the whole thing a bore."

The pastor said, "But it showed you one thing. Worldly psychology can easily come to the conclusion that a Christian is at war with himself. In the Christian there is the new man at war with the old. Non-Christians just have the old man. They may have their struggles, but it isn't the same thing."

"So this means I really can't even be as good as I want to be," Fred observed.

Pastor Martin said, "You cannot be as good as the new man in you wants to be. This is a sorrow and a trial for a Christian, and it won't be cleared up in this life. What you've got is some of both. You've got the flesh, the old sinful nature still at work stirring up all these nasty things that Paul mentions in Galatians 5.

"But you've also got the Holy Spirit stirring up spiritual life, the new man, to all these other things: love, joy, peace, patience, etc. The Holy Spirit does that through his word. But remember that you will not be kept out of heaven by the works of the flesh that still remain, and you won't get into heaven by the fruit of the spirit either."

"I see it better now," said Fred. "Heaven and eternal life are a free gift for Jesus' sake. That's the most important thing to remember."

Pastor Martin finally told Fred, "There are still battles for us to fight. They will go on as long as we live in this sinful world. But the final outcome need never be in doubt for us: victory in Christ."

10. The Man Who Worried About Security

Read 1 Corinthians 1:4-9.

Early one Sunday morning, while it was still dark, Fred and Leona were awakened by the telephone. Fred groped for the phone on the bedside stand. He felt the startled worry that always comes when the phone rings at an odd hour. He said, "Hello?" It was almost a question.

Leona listened and realized that it was Fred's sister. She also realized that something was seriously wrong. Finally Fred said, "Here, Sis, you fill Leona in. I'm getting dressed and then I'm gone. I'll be there in a couple hours."

Fred's sister told Leona about her husband. He had had a sudden heart attack and had been rushed to the hospital. Leona knew that Fred and his sister had always been very close. Since she had married one of Fred's closest buddies, they had all been drawn just that much closer together. There was no question. Fred would be there to help out in any way he could. Leona tried to comfort her sister-in-law as best she could. Then she hung up, intending to help Fred get himself organized and under way.

Leona found her husband in the bathroom trying to brush his teeth while explaining the news to the children. Leona spoke up, "Listen, kids, your uncle is in the hospital, and Dad's going to visit him."

One of them said, "But, Dad, you're gonna miss church."

Fred was wiping his mouth. He said, "Well, sometimes you have to, if it's a real emergency. And this is important enough that I have to leave right now. God wants me to be a good brother, too." Fred made his way out of the bathroom, leaving Leona to explain to the children that they simply did not know yet whether or not their uncle was going to die.

Once he was on the road, Fred thought to himself, "Boy, you never know what's gonna happen next." He thought about his sister and brother-in-law and their children. They had all had such a good time the last time they were together! He thought about the last time he and his sister had had a real heart-to-heart talk. He thought about the time he and his brother-in-law had discussed financial problems.

That just brought back to him all the financial worries that he had had in the past week. Their mortgage was about to be renegotiated. The children needed new shoes. He did not know how he was going to be able to put them through university.

With nobody in the car to hear him, Fred burst out, "Nothing is certain anymore." He realized that he was getting too shook up. He told himself, "Calm down, Fred." He turned on the radio, hoping to find some music that would be easy to listen to. Through the static all he heard was people talking. "Nuts!" he thought to himself. "It's Sunday morning, and I'll probably only get church services and talk shows."

For a few minutes Fred listened to a political talk show. Somebody was pushing policies which he promised would bring security to the nation and the world. He was promising, "If we just have enough of the right kind of education and the right kind of social programs, and if we just take my approach to negotiations with other countries, then everything can work out fine and we can usher in a real golden age of health, peace, and prosperity for everyone."

Fred started fiddling with the dial again. He said, "That's nonsense. We've had more education, more social programs, and more talk than any other century in history. And look at the mess we're in. More people have died in war in this century than in any other."

Fred settled on a different station. He tuned it in because he heard some music for a change. It was not a bad tune, but Fred listened to the words and was not happy. Some guy was promising some girl that they would live in paradise forever if only she would marry him. Fred started fiddling with the dial again. He thought, "That's nonsense. Marriage is good, but it's also hard work. That guy is making his girl friend his god. Wait until they have their first argument — or their first child. And no matter how happily married they are, one of them can die at any time —just like. . . . "

Fred found a station that was playing something that sounded like a hymn. He did not hope for much, but he decided to listen anyway. When the preacher came on, he started talking about a new golden age, the millennium. He promised that it was just around the corner. Jesus would set up his kingdom, with its capital at the earthly Jerusalem and reign on earth for a thousand years. Everything would be wonderful for those who had gotten on the right side of Jesus.

Fred thought, "Nuts to that! Pastor Martin showed us from the Bible just the other week that those guys are all wet. There's gonna be trouble on earth until the end of the world. When Jesus comes back, it will be the end of the world. And Jesus' kingdom is never gonna end."

Fred twisted the dial again. This time he heard a pastor introducing a sermon in a very familiar way: "Grace, mercy, and peace be unto you from God our Father and from our Lord and Savior, Jesus Christ. Amen." The pastor's text was 1 Corinthians 1:4-9. Fred remembered to keep an eye, in fact, both eyes, on the road. But he could almost settle back as if he were in his usual pew at church.

This time what was said made sense out of all that Fred had been worrying about. The pastor read: "I thank my God always on your behalf, for the grace of God which is given you by Jesus Christ; that in every thing ye are enriched by him, in all utterance, and in all knowledge; even as the testimony of Christ was confirmed in you: so that ye come behind in no gift."

The preacher said, "'My dear friends in Christ! We are rich and wealthy. Even if we have financial problems, we are rich. We are rich in the things of the spirit. Why? Because God has given us his word and baptism and the Lord's Supper.

"These are the means of grace, the means by which God gives us what Christ earned on the cross, namely, the forgiveness of sins, eternal life, and salvation. Through these means God gives us faith and strengthens our faith, and he moves us to love him and our neighbor and to grow in that love. All spiritual blessings are ours.

"A few chapters after our text, Paul told the Corinthian Christians, 'All things are yours' (1 Corinthians 3:21). All things are ours. They were earned for us by Christ. They are given to us by God in word and sacrament."

The pastor read: "Waiting for the coming of our Lord Jesus Christ: Who shall also confirm you unto the end, that ye may be blameless in the day of our Lord Jesus Christ."

"Our future is sure and certain, "the pastor continued. "Despite all the dark days in this world, despite all the worries and fears, all the uncertainties, even despite the shadow of death, our future is certain. It is certain because of God's will and God's promises.

"Christ has told us that nobody is going to pluck his sheep out of his hand (John 10:28). Paul tells us elsewhere that God, who has begun a good work in us, is going to perform it until the day of Jesus Christ, the last day (Philip-

58

pians 1:6). We wait. We groan. We are so eager and impatient for that day to come.

"We may have to give up all hope of happiness on this earth, but we will not have to give up the hope of everlasting happiness with the Lord. We wait eagerly for the coming of the Lord Jesus Christ. We can be eager for it, because we know that our many, many sins are forgiven for his sake, because he died on the cross bearing all the guilt of our sinfulness and all our sins. We know that we will stand before him blameless on that day because of what he has done in our place."

The pastor read: "God is faithful, by whom ye were called unto the fellowship of his Son Jesus Christ our Lord."

The pastor said, "We share all these blessings earned by Christ. God has given us this share in them. We did not make ourselves Christian believers. God made us believers and gave each of us these blessings — through the word, through baptism, and through the Lord's Supper. He gave us the faith that believes in the forgiveness of sins earned by Christ on the cross.

"And God is faithful. That means that we have security. Our everlasting joy in salvation does not depend on our faithfulness but on God's faithfulness. He will not change his mind about us. His mind is made up — made up by Christ, who appeased his anger against our sins. We know God's attitude toward us from the word of the gospel, the message of forgiveness. This is also the blessing we receive through baptism and the Lord's Supper — full and free forgiveness for Jesus' sake. This is most certainly true."

Fred thought to himself, "Amen! There is security after all. Something is certain: the forgiveness of sins for Jesus' sake. God isn't mad at us. God is going to make everything work for our benefit — and for our joy. But I sure wish I knew how some things were supposed to be good for us. Sometimes we just have to trust in God."

By this time Fred was getting close to the town where his sister lived. He had to pay attention to road signs, looking for the exit she had told him to take. He was supposed to meet her at the hospital, but he had only a vague idea of how to get there. He finally found it with the help of a friendly policeman. He found his sister in the hospital cafeteria, drinking coffee. She rushed into his arms for a reassuring hug. He asked, "How's your hubby?"

"We still don't know anything for sure," she replied. "The nurse said they'd let me know if there was any news."

"Well, Sis, I have some news, some good news," Fred said. "Let me tell you about it."

While Fred and his sister each sipped a cup of bitter hospital coffee, they drank deeply of the sweet good news of the gospel. While they groaned under the uncertainty of the earthly future, they rejoiced in the security of the everlasting future they and their spouses would share no matter when any of them might die.

While their bodies were saved from weariness only by tension, their spirits were saved from despair by the hope that only the gospel gives. While their minds were tempted to question the wisdom and love of God, their souls rested secure in the forgiveness of sins for Jesus' sake, the only assurance of God's grace. While the flesh shuddered and shrank in fear of the uncertainties of the coming days and weeks and months and years, the spirit stood firm with God-given courage, ready to hear whatever there was to hear from the nurse walking toward their table.

60

11. The Man Who Worried About Persecution

Read 1 Peter 4:12-19.

On Friday evening Fred came home from work all excited. He threw open the door and called to his wife Leona, "Hey, Honey! Guess what?"

Leona came out of the kitchen, still holding a wooden spoon. "What?" she asked.

Fred exulted, "I got a promotion! I'm going to be head of customer relations at the plant!"

"Oh, that's wonderful!" Leona said. "After all those years you worked so hard! Finally they are beginning to recognize you. That's just great!"

Fred told her, "And it means a big, fat raise. Now we can pay some bills and maybe put aside a little bit more for the kids' education."

"And," said Leona, "we can give a bit more to church, don't forget."

"Right," said Fred. "I know I really have to thank God for the new job and the raise. So we'll give a tenth of the raise to church, just as we've been giving a tenth of the rest. But for now, Leona, go turn off the stove and put whatever you were gonna cook back into the refrigerator. I'm taking the whole family out to dinner."

So Fred and Leona and the children had a nice dinner at their favorite family restaurant. They had a very nice evening. In fact, they all felt better all weekend, counting on the security they hoped for from a bigger paycheck.

Fred was in his new office bright and early on Monday morning, looking over the layout and the system. On Tuesday he was beginning to get the feel of things in general. By Wednesday he thought he was getting the hang of the job. He was even beginning to think about an improvement or two in the way the office was run. On Thursday the boss's secretary called Fred's secretary and arranged for Fred to go out to lunch with the boss himself on Friday. Fred congratulated himself. He was really moving up in the corporate structure after starting at the bottom.

About noon on Friday, Fred and his boss caught a cab together. Fred said, "Well, Mr. Blather, it's really nice of you to take me out to lunch."

"Think nothing of it. And call me J. P."

"OK, J. P."

They went to a fancy restaurant. Mr. Blather had settled down for his customary three-martini lunch. Fred drank a glass of wine but turned down anything stronger. Finally, over dessert, Mr. Blather explained to Fred what he wanted him to do. Fred's job was handling relationships with the firm's steady customers. Mr. Blather wanted him to take a new approach, and he explained what it was. But Fred saw right away that it was dishonest.

Fred objected, "But, J. P., that's not a totally accurate way of explaining our company's products and services."

"Yeah," said Mr. Blather. "I know. Haha! But it will get us more business."

"I don't know," Fred hesitated.

"But it can't miss," Mr. Blather insisted. "It'll work. You don't see anything wrong with it, do you?"

Fred swallowed hard. "Sure, it'll work, probably. I don't see anything wrong with it in that respect. But I do see plenty wrong with it as far as ethics go."

"What? You can't be serious."

"Oh, but I am. It's dishonest. It's immoral."

"But it's not illegal. We won't get caught. So who cares?"

"God cares."

"Oh, that's right," Mr. Blather sneered. "You're supposed to be real religious. You'll get over that soon enough when you learn the lay of the land in the real world."

"I hope and pray to God that I never get over it at all," Fred calmly replied. "What you want me to do is against God's will. There is just no way that I can deliberately do something so obviously wrong — not after Jesus Christ came and died for my sins."

"I suppose you never do anything wrong," Mr. Blather sarcastically responded.

"I sin plenty," Fred admitted, "because I'm very weak. But I can't do something so obviously wrong, not when I see clearly how bad it is."

Mr. Blather was getting mad. "Are you preaching at me?"

Fred said, "No, Sir. Ah, yes, Sir. I am, in a way. It's my Christian duty to tell you that this stuff is all wrong. I've gotta be concerned about your soul, too."

"The devil take my soul!" Mr. Blather angrily retorted.

"I wouldn't say that too loudly, if I were you," Fred warned.

Mr. Blather ignored Fred's warning. "Look, Fred, I'll be a nice guy. I'll give you one more chance. Are you gonna do things my way or not?"

"No, J. P., I'm not."

"Then clean out your desk this afternoon. You're through. And don't call me J. P."

Fred cleaned his few belongings out of his desk and headed home in the middle of the afternoon. Losing his job was not his biggest concern. He figured he could handle that pretty well personally. But he was concerned about how disappointed the family would be. He did not really have to go straight home. So he stopped off at the church to see Pastor Martin.

When he was seated in the pastor's study, he said, "Pastor, I've got some bad news." Then he told him the whole story.

"That's not news, Fred."

"You mean, you'd heard about it already?"

"No. I didn't know about your specific situation. But I meant to say that it's not real news. Real news, like something that would make the headlines, is something new or strange or unusual. What you told me is nothing new. Christians have been persecuted that way for thousands of years.

"Look at this text I've been working on for Sunday. St. Peter writes: 'Beloved, think it not strange concerning the fiery trial which is to try you, as though some strange thing happened unto you.' What you're going through is nothing unusual for Christians. Some suffer more, some less, but suffering is very common for Christians."

"Being a Christian can be tough. Life is pretty rough for us, sometimes anyway," Fred agreed.

Pastor Martin said, "That's right. Nobody knew that better than Peter and Paul — except Christ himself. But there's not only sorrow. There's also joy.

"Peter goes on to say: 'But rejoice, inasmuch as ye are partakers of Christ's sufferings; that, when his glory shall be revealed, ye may be glad also with exceeding joy.' Peter tells us — God tells us through Peter — that we can and should be happy anyway. We are suffering the same way Christ suffered. We will also share the joy of his kingdom.

"Our suffering does not earn salvation. Christ's suffering earned us the forgiveness of our sins, life, and salvation. But when we suffer the same way Christ did, then that is a sign that we belong to him. The world persecutes us the same way it did him — and for the same reason."

"Yeah, I suppose I already knew that," Fred agreed, "but I needed to hear it again. In the car just now I was reciting one of my favorite verses: 'I will bless the Lord at all times: his praise shall continually be in my mouth' " (Psalm 34:1).

"That's part of the whole picture, isn't it?" Pastor Martin continued. "Your boss was really blaspheming and insulting Christ — while you were praising him."

"Does every Christian have to go through this sort of thing?" asked Fred.

"The Bible doesn't make it an absolute rule," Pastor Martin replied, "but even in a society where we have freedom of religion, many Christians suffer some kinds of persecution. Children who won't go along with their playmates in harmful kinds of pranks — they often get ridiculed. Young people who won't experiment with drugs, alcohol, and sex — they can be subjected to some pretty strong peer pressure.

"We are bombarded by the Christless culture around us all the time. We aren't thrown to the lions anymore, although people are being imprisoned, tortured, and killed in Communist countries for the name of Christ. But even in the Western world, Christians are persecuted."

"Then is everything a Christian suffers a kind of persecution?" Fred asked.

"No, not really. Everything we suffer as a consequence of confessing and living our Christian faith Jesus describes as bearing the cross," Pastor Martin explained, "but persecution is a narrower category. It refers more to the specific kind of thing you've been going through. Now, if you really had done something wrong and deserved to be fired, then that would not be persecution. But when you suffer for doing right, or for refusing to do wrong, because you are a Christian, then that is persecution."

"I don't exactly know what to think about it," Fred said. "I've never been fired before in my life. But I'm glad I stood up to the boss."

Pastor Martin said, "Look again at what Peter said: 'Yet if any man suffer as a Christian, let him not be ashamed; but let him glorify God on this behalf.' That means that you should be neither ashamed nor proud. You have done nothing to be ashamed of. But you also have no reason to be proud. Oh, you stood up to the boss. But it was God who gave you the strength and the courage to do so. Let's give him the credit."

"That's for sure!" said Fred. "And, really, I don't feel sorry for myself. I feel sorry for Mr. Blather."

Pastor Martin said, "That's the right attitude. You can remember him in your prayers. You might speak to him again or drop him a line to tell him about your concern for his spiritual well-being. But you can't force him to listen to God's word."

"Well," said Fred, "you've helped me to make sense out of this whole thing, Pastor. There's just one more thing."

"What's that?"

Fred looked down at his shoes. "Well, I guess I just don't know what to say to the family. This job meant some security — and it was gonna help pay for the kids' education. Oh, I'll find another job all right, but it might take a while. And I can hardly hope to find another job that pays as well."

Pastor Martin said, "We're finding all our answers in the text for Sunday. Look at this last verse: 'Wherefore let them that suffer according to the will of God commit the keeping of their souls to him in well doing, as unto a faithful Creator.' In other words, Fred, the Bible tells you to trust God for the future. You should commit the keeping of your soul — and your body, for that matter — to God. God will provide. We have the promise that God will take care of us anyway. But here that promise is repeated specifically for your kind of situation."

Fred said, "You know, I don't remember ever hearing that verse before. What does that mean, 'a faithful Creator'?"

Pastor Martin asked, "Are you going to stop loving your children?"

"No way."

"See. If you and I, as sinful as we are, don't stop loving our children, how much more is God going to be faithful in his love for us? He has an awful lot invested in us. He created us in the first place. But in the second place, he has redeemed us by the death of his Son on the cross. In Christ we are new creatures. God has a lot invested in us. You can be sure that he isn't gonna forget about us, stop loving us, or stop taking care of us.

"Now that applies especially in spiritual matters. God will take care of us in earthly matters, too, but sometimes they go by the board a bit — when it's the best thing for us spiritually. But God won't abandon you. He'll see to it that your family's needs are met. You can bank on that."

Fred stood up to leave. "Well, thanks a lot, Pastor. This talk has been really good for me. I'm sorry, though, that I took up so much of your time."

Pastor Martin responded, "Think nothing of it. That's what I'm here for. Besides, I really wasn't getting anywhere trying to write this sermon."

"Well, why not just tell everybody what you told me?"

12. The Man Who Worried About Abortion

Read Psalm 139.

Fred had lost his job. It took him a few weeks, but he did find a new job in his field. He was not making as much money as he might have hoped, but they could get by with careful budgeting. Fred and Leona encouraged each other with the biblical promises that the Lord would provide.

One of the most important things for a new employee to learn is the subtleties of the personal interaction that goes on during that crucial part of the day known as the coffee break. Fred quickly came to understand one of the long-standing traditions at his new place of employment. One of the workers, a man named Horace, would spend the morning coffee break reading the newspaper and grumbling about what he found there. It was also traditional for no one to pay much attention to him.

One morning Horace attracted a lot of attention as he waved the front page and showed everybody the headline: "ABORTION FOES PROTEST AT CITY HOSPITAL." Horace fumed, "Those narrow-minded bigots! Those nasty little so-and-sos! What business do they have trying to tell other people how to run their lives?"

Fred was still a bit hesitant to speak up in this group since he did not yet know the people very well. But he got more and more upset as he realized that most of the people were agreeing with Horace. Nobody was speaking up for the children who were being brutally murdered.

One man was saying, "I've got a friend who's a doctor. And he says that before it's born, it's not a human being. It's just a lump of cells growing in the mother's body. Any woman who wants an abortion should be able to have one!"

That was too much for Fred. He responded, "Wait a minute. There's a lot more to this whole business than that. I read a book where a lot of doctors and scientists say it is a human being from the time it's conceived. And they give a lot of facts to prove it, too."

Horace jumped in again, "See! The so-called experts disagree. So let everybody make up his own mind. Isn't it only fair?"

Fred came back with, "But our pastor says that the Bible teaches that the unborn baby is already a person, somebody God wants protected by the commandment, 'Thou shalt not kill.' "

Horace challenged, "Just show me where the Bible says that God cares about a fetus!"

"Well, I can't — uh — not right off hand."

"Sure! You tell me, Mr. Self-Righteous, would you still be against abortion if an unwanted pregnancy hit close to home?"

Then it was time to go back to work. Fred had never been so glad to see his coffee break end. He worried about it for a while. But then he concentrated on the job he was being paid to do. He would have to figure this one out later.

That evening, while Leona was putting the finishing touches on dinner, Fred told her about the confrontation with Horace. Leona suggested he phone Pastor Martin after dinner. Fred said, "I'll have to. But it sure bothers me that I can't remember the passages we talked about when we covered it in Bible class. I just wish I could have come up with one passage this morning to show Horace that God cares about babies before they are born!"

When dinner was over, before anybody got busy with anything else, Fred picked up his Bible for family devotions. They had been reading through the Psalms, and tonight they were up to Psalm 139.

Fred read: "O Lord, thou hast searched me, and known me." This and the next several verses told Fred and Leona and the children that God knew them, each and every one of them — knew them personally, intimately — better than they knew themselves.

Fred read on: "Whither shall I go from thy spirit? or whither shall I flee from thy presence? . . . If I take the wings of the morning, and dwell in the uttermost parts of the sea; even there shall thy hand lead me, and thy right hand shall hold me." Fred paused and thought, "You can't get away from God. That would be bad news if he were mad at me. But I know the good news that God's isn't mad at me, that my sins are forgiven because of Jesus' life and because of his death on the cross. So it means I'm never anywhere where God isn't with me to bless me."

"Thou hast covered me in my mother's womb. I will praise thee; for I am fearfully and wonderfully made: marvellous are thy works; and that my soul knoweth right well. My substance was not hid from thee, when I was made in secret. . . . Thine eyes did see my substance, yet being unperfect; and in thy book all my members were written. . . . How precious also are thy thoughts unto me, O God! How great is the sum of them!"

The different members of the family naturally had different degrees of knowledge about the growth of a baby in the womb. But they were all impressed with the great care with which God fashions a baby before it is born. It meant something to each of them, but it meant just a little more to Leona than to the others.

"Surely thou wilt slay the wicked, O God: depart from me therefore, ye bloody men." Fred thought, "Capital punishment is the only just punishment for murder — especially for abortion."

Fred concluded the reading of the Psalm: "Search me, O God, and know my heart: try me, and know my thoughts: And see if there be any wicked way in me, and lead me in the way everlasting."

Then Fred led the family in prayer: "O Lord God! Please stop the murder of babies in our country. And please help us to speak out against abortion whenever we have the opportunity. And please keep us from being self-righteous. Keep us from being blind to our own sins, but always comfort us with the message of the forgiveness of sins for Jesus' sake. In his name we pray. Amen."

Just as Fred finished praying, there was a knock on the door. It was Fred's brother Bill. He was all upset and out of breath. He said, "Fred, I've gotta talk to you, alone."

So Fred and Bill went into the den. Fred said, "I take it you didn't drop in just to chat."

"No. It's pretty serious," Bill said. After a pause, he went on, "It's Suzanne. She's pregnant."

Fred was shocked. Suzanne was Bill's oldest daughter, so she was Fred's niece. The whole family had always thought the world of Suzanne. And here she was, an unwed mother. All Fred could say for the moment was, "That is serious."

Bill told Fred as much as he knew. Then Fred asked, "Well, uh, does she know she did wrong?"

"Oh, yes," said Bill. "She's really torn up over it now. She feels terribly guilty."

Fred said, "Well, then, you can certainly assure her of the forgiveness of sins. Jesus died for all sins. God has obviously brought her to repentance. Of course, she should talk to the pastor and hear the gospel from him, too."

"Oh, no," said Bill.

"Why not?" asked Fred.

"Well," said Bill, "we want to keep it quiet."

Fred said, "We both know you can't keep a baby quiet."

Bill studied the floor between his shoes and said, "No. I mean, her mother and I want her to have an abortion. But she won't hear of it. Said she'd feel like a murderer. That's really why I came over here, Fred. You're her favorite uncle. Can't you talk some sense into her?"

Fred said, "She's not the one who needs a talking to right now." So Fred went over Psalm 139 with his brother Bill. Bill started to get a little bit angry, but he was also shaken up as he began to see that abortion was against God's law and will.

But Bill was a bit too stubborn to admit that Fred was right. That was how Bill might have expressed it to himself. Really, he did not want to admit that God was right. So Bill tried to change the subject. He said, "But Suzanne has brought disgrace on our whole family. I'm so mad I'd like to kick her out of the house. She is eighteen."

"Well, if she needs a place to stay, she's welcome here," Fred offered. "She did wrong, but she knows that now. She also knows that two wrongs don't make a right. I'm not butting in, Bill. You got me involved. I know I've gotta do anything I can to prevent a murder."

Bill left in a huff, but Fred was glad he had said what he had said. Now he could talk to Horace the next day. Not only could he show Horace where the Bible said that God cares about unborn babies, but he could also tell Horace about the courage God's word gives people to deal with problems that hit close to home.

13. The Man Who Worried About a Delinquent

Read 1 Corinthians 9:24 to 10:5.

Fred had an old friend named Louie. Fred and Louie had gone through school together. They had been confirmed together. They had been in the church's youth group together. And they had dropped out of active church membership about the same time. Fred had been brought back into the fold. Louie had not.

Fred had worried about Louie. They still lived in the same town, but they did not see each other very often. One Friday evening Fred was out picking up something for Leona. In the store Fred went around the end of an aisle and bumped right into Louie. They greeted each other like the old friends they were. Then Fred said, "Hey, Louie, if you got a couple minutes, let's grab a cup of coffee."

They went to a nearby coffee shop and started talking over old times. All the while they talked about the good old days, Fred was still worried about Louie's spiritual welfare. Finally Fred said, "Say, Louie, uh, you know, the wife and the kids and I, we're all going to church again, regular, like in the old days."

"Oh?"

"Yeah. We go every Sunday we can. Get a lot out of it, too. Say, I'd sure like to see you coming out again, too."

Louie said, "Don't hold your breath. I'm not really interested anymore."

"What are you doing that's more important?"

"Oh, this and that. I'm just too busy."

"Like, with what?"

"Oh, you know, work and sports and the family and all that."

"But shouldn't you take some time to see about your spiritual well-being, Louie? I mean, that's an important part of life, too, isn't it?"

"Sure. But don't bug me about it, Fred. Look, God forgives sins, right? So don't we have it made? We aren't saved by good works. So why should I bother about going to church and all that stuff? I mean, I was baptized. I was confirmed. I don't have to worry, right?"

"Well," said Fred, "I don't know."

"Sure," said Louie. "Hey, I gotta go."

That ended the discussion, but it did not end Fred's concern for Louie. He just did not know what to say or do next.

The next morning was Saturday. Fred lingered over his second cup of coffee at breakfast. He asked Leona why their son Ned had not showed up for breakfast. Ned, at fourteen, was usually the first one up, full of energy and more plans than he could possibly accomplish.

"I don't know. I called him, and he just sort of groaned," Leona answered.

Just then Ned walked sleepily into the kitchen. He slumped into a chair and asked, "Dad, am I too young to feel old?"

"I think so, Son. Wait a few years for that. Why?"

"I'm just sore, I guess. The coach is making us all work extra hard lately, and I'm bushed."

"Well, it just takes time to get used to it. You'll get there," Fred assured his son.

That afternoon, Fred and Ned went out to run a few errands. When they were done, Fred suggested a hot fudge sundae, Ned's favorite. But Ned said, "No thanks, Dad."

"Are you feeling all right?"

"Sure. But the coach said to watch the sweets. You know, Dad, I'm beginning to wonder if it's worth it to go to practice and all. What do you think?"

Fred told him, "You know that athletics is not the most important thing in the world — but you can learn some good things from it. It can help you stay in shape. I think it's a good thing as long as you don't get reckless and get hurt. But to be good, really good, you have to make some sacrifices. Only you can decide whether it's worth it for you."

"Do the professional athletes have to do all this practicing and stuff, and watch their weight?" asked Ned.

"The ones that are gonna be champs do — especially if they want to stay on top very long. They make a lot of sacrifices to win," Fred explained.

Something clicked in Fred's mind. He thought to himself, "Why didn't I say that to Louie last night? The Bible talks that way. If an athlete can make sacrifices for earthly prizes, we can certainly make sacrifices and go into training for heavenly prizes. The Bible does talk that way — but wait a minute! Doesn't that make it all works righteousness again? Doesn't that mean that we get to heaven by our own effort? What does the Bible say?"

Fred was unable to put it out of his mind. He wanted to phone Pastor Martin, but they were having guests that evening. Fred just did not have the time. But the next day was Sunday. There was a coffee hour after the church service, so Fred took advantage of it to corner Pastor Martin with this question: Was an athlete's training and competing similar to the Christian life?

Pastor Martin answered in the affirmative and pulled out his pocket New Testament to show Fred 1 Corinthians

9:24-27: "Know ye not that they which run in a race run all, but one receiveth the prize? So run, that ye may obtain. And every man that striveth for the mastery is temperate in all things. Now they do it to obtain a corruptible crown; but we an incorruptible. I therefore so run, not as uncertainly; so fight I, not as one that beateth the air: But I keep under my body, and bring it into subjection; lest that by any means, when I have preached to others, I myself should be a castaway."

Fred asked further, "But doesn't that make works necessary for salvation? You always say that works are not necessary for salvation."

Pastor Martin explained: "Works are not necessary for salvation, Fred. You know the passages like Ephesians 2:8,9: 'For by grace are ye saved through faith; and that not of yourselves: it is the gift of God: Not of works, lest any man should boast.' But what Paul is talking about here in 1 Corinthians is not doing good works for salvation. He is talking about the Christian life as a struggle, a struggle in which discipline is needed."

Fred said, "I don't get it."

Pastor Martin explained, "OK. Christ has provided completely for our salvation. He died on the cross for the forgiveness of all our sins. And the Holy Spirit has brought this salvation to us in the word and in baptism and in the Lord's Supper. And He has brought us to faith.

"But the point here is that we are still in the middle of a struggle. We are struggling against the devil, the world, and our own flesh, and we are in danger. That's the main point of the context that follows what I read. The next chapter talks about the people of Israel in the Old Testament — how they were delivered from slavery in Egypt in a miraculous way that they all saw — yet many of them fell into gross idolatry and were killed by God in the desert."

"Then it isn't a matter of our salvation being something we win or deserve," Fred observed.

"Pastor Martin went on, "That's right. Salvation is a gift, a totally free gift, for Jesus' sake. When Paul compares his struggles to an athlete's, he is not saying that he is racing against other Christians, nor that he is boxing with other Christians. Our competition, our opposition is not our fellow Christians but the devil, the world, and our own flesh."

"Then does a Christian have to live in fear that he is going to fall away?" Fred wondered.

Pastor Martin said, "Not exactly. Remember, we have other promises, too. St. Peter talked about Christians being 'kept by the power of God through faith unto salvation' (1 Peter 1:5). And Jesus promised about his sheep: 'My sheep hear my voice, and I know them, and they follow me: And I give unto them eternal life; and they shall never perish, neither shall any man pluck them out of My hand' " (John 10:27,28).

"I don't get it," said Fred.

Pastor Martin went on, "The Bible teaches both — that we are to rely on God to keep us in the faith and to preserve us for salvation, but also that we are still in danger. If anybody falls away from the faith, it is his own fault. But if anybody is kept in the faith, then God gets the credit."

So Fred told Pastor Martin about his talk with Louie. He asked the pastor for advice. Pastor Martin said, "I'll go see Louie, but you should talk to him again, too. What Louie needs to be told is that he's in pretty sad shape, spiritually. His soul hasn't had the proper nutrition for a long time, if he's been getting any spiritual food at all. He's out of training. That's his own fault, and he needs to be told so. When he realizes that — and even that conviction is something which God must bring about in him — then he should be told again about the full and free forgiveness that Jesus earned for us by dying on the cross for all human sin."

"I get it now," said Fred. "But he would still need the warning not to let his work or his recreation become an idol, a false god, and draw him away from God's word again."

"We all need that warning," said Pastor Martin. "The Israelites had no excuse when they fell into idolatry. We need to remember, though, that if we are preserved, God gets the credit — for it is all his doing. But if we are lost, we get the blame — for that would be our doing. That warning is sometimes in place. But the main point of the Bible is bringing us to trust God for all our needs, but most of all for our salvation. We are not trustworthy. But God is trustworthy, and that is why even a warning should not make us worry."

14. The Man Who Worried About Temptation

Read Matthew 4:1-11.

Fred had a friend named Sam. Through Fred, Sam had gotten involved in the Lutheran church. He had taken adult confirmation class and been confirmed. He was really quite active in the church. He usually went to all of the church's services and activities. In Advent he was in every Wednesay evening service. But when Lent came, Sam was not sure about going to the Wednesday evening services.

Fred asked Sam whether he was going to the service on Ash Wednesday. Sam told him that he was too busy. The truth was that Sam was quite a sports fan. He especially loved hockey. He was closely following his favorite team and his favorite players. A big game was being televised on Ash Wednesday, and Sam had been invited over to Dick's house to watch the game on Dick's big new color television set.

It turned out that Dick did not only want to watch hockey. During a break in the game, he turned to Sam and said, "Hey, listen, Sam! I've got a real good business deal I want you to go in on with me. See, we'd open up our own shop."

Dick got very excited as he outlined the whole plan for going into business, mixing his comments with cheers and groans at the rest of the hockey game. Afterwards they continued to talk about it. Dick was really pushing to get Sam to go along.

Sam had to admit that it was a very interesting proposition. The first temptation was the profit that might be made. Dick had some glowing promises about how much they were going to take in. Sam was the kind of guy who worried about making ends meet anyway, and his finances were not in very good shape in general.

But Sam also tended to be the cautious type. He said, "Look, Dick, uh, it seems like a good deal, but it's not really a sure thing. You know, we could lose our shirts!"

So Dick said, "Oh, Sam, nothing ventured, nothing gained. Sure, it's taking a chance, but, say, you're a church-goer, aren't you? Don't you believe that God takes care of his own? So you do some praying on top of working hard. Everything will be fine. 'God helps those who help themselves.' "

"Well," said Sam, "it still wouldn't be easy."

"Oh, I know," said Dick. "But we'll work hard, real hard. It'll take lots of time, especially at first. There won't be much time for anything else. We'll keep our old jobs for a while and moonlight. We'll work Saturdays and Sundays. This will be our number one priority. It's important. We'll make successes of ourselves, all right, no matter what it takes."

"I still don't know," said Sam, "but it's awfully tempting."

"Sure!" said Dick. "Hey, think it over. We'll talk about it again in a couple of days."

Sam thought it over for a couple of days all right, but the next time he discussed it, it was with Fred, not with Dick. Sam had been invited to have dinner with Fred and Leona on Friday night. Pastor Martin was also there. All during dinner, Sam was preoccuppied. Pastor Martin did not mention it, thinking it might be something private. But over coffee Fred finally said, "Sam, what's bothering you?"

So Sam told them all about the business deal that Dick had suggested. Then he asked, "Any advice?"

Fred said, "Sounds risky to me. What do you think, Pastor?"

"Well, I don't like to give business advice," Pastor Martin replied. "I don't claim to know much about these things. But I will say that according to the Bible, Sam, you should use your time and money in reponsible ways that will help people — and, of course, not in any way that would go against God's will. That's the basis on which you should make your decision."

Sam said, "Well, there are dangers involved in any business deal, but there's a lot of money to be made. The money is really tempting right now. I'm not broke, but the old bank account sure could use a boost."

"Maybe 'tempting' is the right word," Pastor Martin commented. "Remember when Jesus was tempted by Satan. He hadn't eaten a thing in forty days, and then Satan challenged him to turn some stones into bread. But Jesus quoted the Old Testament: 'Man shall not live by bread alone, but by every word that proceedeth out of the mouth of God' " (Deuteronomy 8:3).

"Does that mean that we shouldn't work and should just let God feed us?" asked Sam.

"No," Fred said, "because the Bible also says, 'If any would not work, neither should he eat' " (2 Thessalonians 3:10).

Pastor Martin said, "That's true. God's word teaches us to work for a living — but also to trust God. We should work and be responsible, but we shouldn't worry. And especially we shouldn't let worries about money direct or control our lives."

"I know that's right," Sam agreed, "but Dick said something I couldn't answer. He seemed to say that if I trusted God, I should take a chance on this deal. Now that didn't sound quite right, but I didn't know what to say. I mean, he had me real interested. I just didn't know what to say."

Fred said, "Pastor, doesn't that fit in with another temptation that Jesus faced?"

Pastor Martin suggested, "Why don't you keep talking, Fred?"

So Fred went on, "Well, Satan tried to get Jesus to jump off the temple with the idea that God's angels would keep him from getting hurt. He even quoted the Old Testament, one of the Psalms, wasn't it? But Jesus wouldn't go for it. He quoted the Bible, too. What was it he said?"

Pastor Martin said, "Jesus quoted the passage, 'Thou shalt not tempt the Lord thy God' (Deuteronomy 6:16). That means that God's promises of help don't mean we can be irresponsible or take foolish chances."

"So that's just what I should have told Dick," Sam concluded. "Trust in God's help doesn't mean I don't have to think things over and make careful decisions. But Dick wasn't being totally reckless. I mean, he was talking about working real hard, working weekends, being a real success. He promised he'd make success in this business his number one priority."

Pastor Martin said, "That sounds suspicious."

"What do you mean?" asked Sam.

Pastor Martin explained, "It reminds me of the third temptation Jesus faced. Satan promised him uncontested control of the world if Jesus would just once bow down and worship Satan."

"I don't see the connection," said Sam. "Dick doesn't go to church, but I'm sure he doesn't worship Satan."

"That's not what I mean," said the pastor. "The point is that Satan tried to tempt Jesus with worldly power, just as Dick is tempting you with success. And the price of that success might just be idolatry — not the idolatry of literally bowing down to worship someone or something but the idolatry of putting money ahead of God."

"That's right." Sam admitted. "Dick wanted me to commit my Sundays to the project."

Pastor Martin said, "That's only part of the picture, but it's an important part."

"But wait a minute," Fred interrupted. "Can we really compare Jesus' temptations to ours? I mean, he's God. He couldn't sin, could he?"

Pastor Martin said, "You're right. Because He's God, he could not be imperfect. But he is also truly human, so he was really tempted. It was a real contest with Satan, even though the outcome was never in doubt. So the biggest difference between Jesus' temptation and ours is that he never gave in. Sometimes we Christians give in because we are still weak and the old sinful nature is still with us in this life.

"Jesus also went through these temptations for us, in our place. It was all part of his keeping God's law for us. His obedience to his Father was also something he offered to earn the forgiveness of sins for us. And it was important for his sacrifice on the cross that he really was the spotless Lamb of God, not having been guilty of any sins of his own. So it is all part of the picture of our sins being forgiven because of Jesus' total obedience to the Father in life and death. Satan tempts Christians not to be Christians. But he tempted Christ not to be Christ, not to be our Savior. Jesus did not give in. He did save us."

"When you see it all fit together like that, our temptations are a lot less, uh, less tempting," Sam concluded.

"Or maybe it's that Jesus gives us the power to overcome temptation," Fred commented.

"We shouldn't mess around with temptation," Pastor Martin warned. "But when it comes, the gospel, the message of God's love and grace and forgiveness in Christ, gives us the power to resist."

15. The Man Who Worried About Freedom

Read Galatians 4:21-31.

The Lutheran church to which Fred belonged decided to have a big mission festival so that every member would learn more about mission work and would support it more eagerly. It would be encouraging for Christian people to see how the gospel was being brought to those who were still caught in false religions. Fred was asked to be the chairman of the committee to organize the whole festival.

Fred was reluctant to accept the position, but he found it more and more exciting as he himself learned more about mission work and as the plans took shape. One thing that everybody wanted was to have a missionary come as a guest speaker at one of the evening festivities. Pastor Martin found out that an experienced missionary from one of the third-world countries was on furlough in their area and would be available to speak. Missionary Braun gladly accepted the invitation.

Leona suggested that Missionary Braun should enjoy their hospitality while he would be in town. Fred picked him up at the airport in the afternoon, but they really did not have time to talk about anything until dinner that evening.

After they had gotten to know each other a bit, Leona asked Missionary Braun, "What is the most difficult problem you experience in getting the people to give up their old way of life? Is it getting them to give up their superstitions?"

Missionary Braun answered, "No, their superstitions are not that hard to get rid of, at least, not for the people I work with. Once they are converted to Christianity, it's very clear to them that their old religion was from the devil, from Satan himself. They reject it lock, stock, and barrel. The hardest thing is to get them to give up polygamy."

Fred and Leona's little girl asked, "Poly-what?"

"That's when there's more than one mommy in the same family," Fred explained.

The little girl said, "I wouldn't like that!"

Leona asked, "Didn't they see anything wrong with polygamy?"

Missionary Braun answered, "No, they didn't. But we finally got them to give it up when their understanding of Scripture progressed far enough."

Fred said, "I've often wondered about that. Where does the Bible forbid polygamy? Not that I have any interest in it myself," he hastened to add.

Missionary Braun said, "Well, it says that the two shall be one flesh. It doesn't say that three or four shall be one flesh."

"But some of the men in the Old Testament had more than one wife," Leona commented.

Missionary Braun said, "Yes, but I remember that one of my seminary professors pointed out how all of them had trouble in their families because of it."

That evening Missionary Braun spoke on the topic, "Bringing the Gospel to the Heathen." He showed slides of his own work. He ended the presentation by summarizing the gospel message which he brought to the unbelievers. He especially emphasized that his task was to use God's word to call them out of darkness into God's marvelous light, to call them from the slavery of sin, fear, and superstition to the glorious liberty of the children of God.

Then there was a question-and-answer session. First one of the congregation members got up and asked, "What is the hardest thing to get across to these people?"

Missionary Braun answered quickly, "The hardest thing to get across to them is that we are saved by God's grace in Christ, not by our own works. People naturally tend to think in terms of earning things from God by good works. And these people are taught from little on that that is the only way.

"We are coming with a totally new message to them, something they have never heard or dreamt of before. We come and tell them that we have God's favor because of Jesus' life and death. We tell them that our salvation is earned by Christ's works, not by our works. Bringing them to this faith is not something which we can do — after all, we could not bring ourselves to faith either. In their case as well as in ours, we give all the glory and the credit to God. He does it through his word. That's the only way."

Then someone else got up with a comment. This was not a member of the congregation but someone from the community, for the public had been invited. This man stood up and objected, "Now wait a minute. Let me see if I got this straight. It sounds to me like you're going out there telling these people that God does it all for their salvation."

Missionary Braun said, "That's right."

The man continued, "But aren't you telling them that they have to do their part?"

"No," Missionary Braun responded, "our message, the Bible's message, is that God did it all and does it all. There is

86

no human credit or glory for salvation. The Father sent the Son to live a perfect life for all mankind and to die a perfect death, suffering the penalty for all the sins of all mankind. Christ appeased the wrath of God against all our sins. And the gospel that we preach is the good news that this has been accomplished. The Holy Spirit uses this message to create faith in people's hearts, the confidence that their sins really are forgiven for Jesus' sake. That is the word that the church is to proclaim to the world."

The man objected again, "But wait a minute! I've heard a lot of preachers in my time. But this is the first time I've ever heard anybody say this. Every preacher I know says we've gotta do our part. We've gotta do our best to live a good life. And we've gotta accept Jesus into our hearts and lives. We've gotta make Jesus our Savior and Lord. And then we've gotta do what we can to live the way he wants us to."

Missionary Braun said, "You know, we were just getting into this at the dinner table this evening before we came to church. Did you know that Abraham had two sons? One was named Ishmael, and his mother was a slave named Hagar. The other was free, and his mother was free. That was Isaac, and his mother was Sarah.

"That really represents the kind of conflict I face on the mission fields and, if I may say so, the kind of disagreement we seem to have here tonight. Most religions, and sometimes even what is preached in the name of Christianity, really make us God's slaves, not God's children. All religions that teach that we have to earn God's love, God's favor, God's grace, all those religions, by whatever name they are called, are really slave religions.

"The people I preach to have come from a slave religion. The Jews of Paul's day had a slave religion. Many people who call themselves Christians have not yet seen the light. They are still slaves."

The man objected again, "But don't you believe that we should serve God?"

Missionary Braun answered, "Yes, of course! But there are different attitudes about serving God. Some people try to serve God because they are scared of him, because they see him only as the harsh taskmaster or only as a judge who is eager to condemn them. They may do some things outwardly to try to please God, but their heart is not in it. Really, they hate God for being their slaveowner. And when you strip away the masks, that is what every religion is — except the Christian religion.

"In Christianity we teach that we are God's free children. He has chosen us because he loved us. He has given us the new birth and the new life of faith in Christ. He has given his Son to live and die for us, to earn our salvation. He has given us his Holy Spirit to bring us to faith in Christ and to keep us in that faith through the word and the sacraments. We serve God because we love him, not because we are afraid of him. We love him because we know how much he has done for us. We fear him only as children respect their father — not as the murderer fears the hangman.

"So we who are children of God through faith in Christ are free people. We serve God willingly and freely because he has saved us. The church is God's kingdom. We are in that kingdom as full, free, first-class citizens. The church is God's house — and we are there as members of the family, not as slaves or hired help who are afraid of the boss and come to him hat in hand. We are children of God, and Jesus says that the children are free (Matthew 17:26)."

At that point the man got huffy. He said, "Look. I came with money in my pocket, intending to give it to support your work, if I liked what I heard. But what you're saying is just wrong. You make salvation mighty cheap."

Missionary Braun answered, "Our salvation was very expensive for Christ. But for us it is not cheap, it is free."

At that point the questioner left in a real huff. The exchange between him and the missionary did put a damper on questions and comments for a short time. But

Missionary Braun showed that he was not overly disturbed, and eventually the discussion picked up.

Later, over coffee, Fred and Pastor Martin were speaking with the missionary. Fred said to him, "I want to apologize for what happened before. I never expected anything like that. Maybe we shouldn't have opened it up to the public."

"No," said Missionary Braun. "There is no need to apologize. I am always glad when something like this is open to the public. It should be. Listen, what happened tonight didn't really bother me. Remember, I have preached to groups where the men were all still carrying spears and machetes."

Fred said, "I just don't understand what that guy's problem was."

"Oh, I do," Missionary Braun said. "It's really the same problem I face in the foreign mission field. Paul faced it in his day. You face it here as we saw tonight. There are people who want to be saved by the law. They want that either because they think it has to be that way — after all, you have to work for everything else you get — or because they are proud and want at least some of the credit for their salvation."

Pastor Martin commented, "That's really true. And I can't say which is harder — preaching to people in an area where Christianity is something totally new, or talking to people here at home who think they already know all about Christianity and still want to be saved by the law instead of the gospel."

16. The Man Who Worried About the Victorious Christian Life

Read 1 John 5:4,5.

Fred and Leona were having a rough time in several ways. For one thing, they were having trouble making ends meet financially. They had some unexpected expenses, and there was inflation. They were also deeply concerned about the kinds of friends some of the children were making.

Fred himself was not well physically. Nothing definite was wrong. He simply felt run down. The physician had only given him some vague advice about diet. But he still had not had the energy to do much with the family after work. He had not gotten around to several jobs that Leona considered pretty important. For that and other reasons, Fred and Leona had tangled a time or two. They really had not argued often in the course of their marriage, but lately Fred thought that Leona was getting more irritable, while Leona thought that Fred did not seem to care much about anything anymore.

So the family was not happy. Then they got some good news. Fred's Uncle Bill was coming to town on a business trip and planned to spend the weekend with Fred and family. Everybody loved Uncle Bill. He was from the branch of the family that lived in Texas, and he would regale everybody with western stories that might or might not be exactly true.

Fred was happy to meet Uncle Bill at the airport. Bill got off the plane with a smile as wide as a longhorn's horns are long. That and his ten-gallon hat made it easy for Fred to spot him. He was the picture of health and the image of energy. He shook Fred's hand so hard that it hurt. Then he slapped his nephew so hard on the back that he lost his breath for a moment. But Uncle Bill never lost his breath. He barely stopped talking all the way home in the car.

Everybody was excited to see Uncle Bill. There was a lot of chatter and banter during dinner and throughout the evening. Finally the children were persuaded to go to bed. Uncle Bill was still going strong. Fred and Leona also turned in and left Bill watching a western movie on the late show.

After breakfast the next morning, the children seemed to disappear for a few minutes and left Fred and Leona and Uncle Bill at the table drinking their coffee. Bill turned to Fred and said, "Fred, boy, what's wrong?"

"What do you mean?"

"Why, boy, there's been a bit of chuckling since I showed up, but you can't fool me. It was all just coverin' over gloom thicker than a Texas sandstorm. The kids ain't exactly tickled pink with Ma and Pa. And I can see that you and Leona ain't exactly billing and cooing like the lovebirds you used to be. So just 'fess up and tell ole Uncle Bill what's wrong."

Fred started to admit a couple of things, "Well, you're exaggerating, Uncle Bill, but it is true that we have been having trouble with one or two of the children. And we've got some money worries right now. It isn't serious. We're all just a bit preoccupied. That's all. You know, that kind of thing gets on people's nerves. It's nothing to worry about." He glanced at Leona to see her reaction.

Leona seconded what he had said: "I have to admit that we may have fallen into some pattern of unhappiness around here. But it's normal. We'll come out of it. We all still believe in Christ, and we know that things will work out, even if we do have trouble in this life."

Fred was glad to hear Leona say that. One of them should have said it to the other much sooner. It would be a good point to make at family devotions that evening — something which had unfortunately been forgotten in the excitement of the previous evening.

But Uncle Bill was shaking his head. He was not satisfied with what Leona had said. He said, "Well, folks, back home the Missus and I always listen to this preacher on TV. I've heard a heap of preachers in my time, but he's gotta be the best of the bunch. He's always saying that the Christian life should be victorious. In fact, he just wrote a book with a title about that, something about 'victorious Christian living.' I don't know the exact title. I got a free copy the last time I sent him a check.

"Now, see, he would say that you two are living like defeated Christians. Why, you must not be doing the right things. You gotta do something about it. You gotta make Jesus the Lord of your life. If you do that, and if you live right, why, God is gonna shower down blessings just to fill all them dry river beds in your lives right up to overflowing.

"If you make Jesus the Lord of your life, and if you live up to your committment to him, then you're gonna have health and wealth and your whole family is gonna be just as happy as an ol' hog in a new mudhole."

"Uncle Bill, you don't really believe that, do you?" asked Fred.

"Why, Fred," Uncle Bill replied, "I thought you were a believer. Besides, who's the one with all the problems? Not me, no sir! I'm in the pink of condition. And I'm so solvent, it's disgusting. Why, when the bank needs money, they come to me. And the Missus and I, why, we ain't never been happier in all our forty years of marriage. So you tell me why you don't believe in the victorious Christian life."

"Where does the Bible talk about this kind of thing?" Leona asked.

"Well, uh, come to think of it, I don't rightly know," Uncle Bill admitted, "but, hey, this preacher says it all the time on TV. And it's working for me. Ain't that proof enough?"

Just then one of the children burst into the room shouting, "Mommy, Daddy, Uncle Bill, you gotta come outside and see what we found!" So they all trooped outside. After a bit, Fred and Leona left Uncle Bill to play with the children.

Nobody could have said for certain who was having more fun, the children or their uncle. But Fred and Leona had things on their minds. Leona was not worried about what Uncle Bill had said because she was satisfied with her first answer to him. So she went to get started preparing the huge dinner for all the relatives who were coming over to see Uncle Bill that evening. Eventually the children caught on and started helping her — except for the youngest one, who got the job of entertaining Uncle Bill.

Meanwhile Fred was asking himself some hard questions. He went into the study and phoned Pastor Martin, but there was no answer. So Fred leaned back in his chair and tried to puzzle things out for himself. In a way, what Uncle Bill had said made sense. But he could not forget that Uncle Bill had not been able to tell Leona where it was in the Bible. He also knew that Pastor Martin would have had something from the Bible to show him.

But Fred did not know at first how to find a relevant Bible passage. Then he remembered his concordance, a book that has Bible passages listed under key words. So he looked up *victory*. There seemed to be a few references to military victories. Then his eyes lit on 1 John 5:4. The concordance gave just a part of the verse, but it read, "This is the victory." Fred figured that verse might answer his questions.

Quickly he looked up 1 John 5:4. Then he read the whole chapter. He was excited because the answer was right there. He knew what to say at family devotions that evening. He made a few notes before Leona called them for lunch.

After lunch, various relatives began showing up with bowls of this and that for the evening meal. Everybody who came in had no trouble hearing where Uncle Bill was. His audience got larger, and his tales got taller. He kept everybody entertained until dinner time.

After the happy but loud meal, Fred announced that it was time for devotions. Even those relatives who were not churchgoers could hardly object. Fred had a captive audience. He began: "In the name of the Father and of the Son and of the Holy Ghost. Amen. Tonight we are going to consider, 1 John 5:4,5: 'For whatsoever is born of God overcometh the world: and this is the victory that overcometh the world, even our faith. Who is he that overcometh the world, but he that believeth that Jesus is the Son of God?'

"I'm really glad you're all here for devotions because I have something important to say. We all hear about one another's problems. And we all care for each other, some more, some less. We all know it should be more. But let's talk about our problems. Our troubles get us down. We can get down on ourselves and down on others. And sometimes we have to admit that we aren't doing such a good job with life. We are sinners, whether we like to hear it or not.

"We know we are sinners. We are tempted to think that we are losers rather than winners because of our sins. But that is just not so. No Christian, no believer in Christ is a loser. Every believer in Christ is a winner.

"That's what these Bible passages mean. Everyone who is born of God — born of water and the word in baptism —every Christian believer, that is, is a winner. He overcomes the world. Faith itself is the victory. By faith in Christ, he is a winner.

"What does that mean? Well, that's a good question. Faith in Christ doesn't put food on the table or clothes on your back or a roof over your head. Faith in Christ does not promise health and wealth and success on earth. Faith in Christ does not make you a world-beater in those ways.

"Faith by itself is nothing, but we are talking about faith in Christ. Christ is the real winner, the victor, the conqueror. We're talking about faith in the Son of God, who came to earth to save us sinners. He suffered and died on the cross for our sins. That really looked like a defeat, not a victory, but He turned it into a mighty big victory because he rose from the dead.

"Faith in Christ believes that he died because we were sinners and he was guilty with our guilt. Faith in Christ believes that he rose again because he had paid the full penalty for our sins and our sins really were forgiven. Even those of you who don't go to church every week should have heard this sometime when you were there.

"So even though we have trials and troubles, we are winners. Our sins are forgiven for Jesus' sake, and God isn't angry with us anymore. So even the things that seem so bad are somehow going to work out for our good. And we are winners, we believers are winners, especially because we have eternal life and salvation. This victory has been won for all of us, and every believer has it. So everything that seems like a defeat for a believer, well, we just have to wait to see how it is all going to be part of the victory that every believer has in Christ."

Fred said a prayer and the Lord's Prayer and blessed everyone in the name of the Triune God. Slowly some conversation got started again. Fred looked at Uncle Bill. For a change, he seemed to be thinking instead of talking.

17. The Boy Who Worried About Confirmation

Read Acts 2:42.

Fred's son Ned was confirmed late in the spring. A few weeks after confirmation, on a Saturday evening, Fred decided to take the dog for a walk. Ned wanted to go along. So Fred said, "Sure! The more, the merrier."

While they walked, they talked of this and that. Then Ned said, "Uh, Dad, can I ask you something?"

"Sure, Son, anything."

"Well, some of the guys are going fishing tomorrow morning down at the pond. Can I go along?"

"Son, do you remember what day tomorrow is?"

"Well, it's Sunday."

"And what do we do on Sunday?"

"You used to play golf."

"Yes, Son, I remember. But that wasn't the right thing to do. I wasn't very close to the Lord in those days. Isn't it really a lot nicer for the whole family now that we all go to church together?"

Ned admitted that it was better. Then he added, "But the Lord forgave you for all those Sundays you missed church, didn't he?"

Fred answered, "Yes, Jesus died for those sins, too. But since I know that he had to die on the cross for my sins, and since I know how much God loves me — well, since I know all that, it sort of takes away a lot of the desire to sin. Do you see what I mean?"

"Yes, I guess so," Ned admitted "but this would only be one Sunday. I promise I'll go to church the next Sunday."

"That's how it got started with me," Fred said. "I just wanted to play golf with my buddies one Sunday. Then it sort of dragged on into a month, and then the whole summer. Pretty soon, I wasn't going at all."

Ned pleaded, "But, Dad, I promise that I'll only miss one Sunday. Isn't my promise good enough?"

Fred asked, "Didn't you make a promise a few weeks ago, in church? Remember?"

Ned asked, "You mean, when I was confirmed?"

His father answered, "That's right. Do you remember what you promised?"

Ned hesitated, but then he replied, "Yes, Sir. I promised that I would hear God's word preached and go to the Lord's Supper often. I promised to be an active member of the church."

His father asked, "Do you remember your confirmation verse?"

The son said, "Yes. It was Acts 2 — something or other, wasn't it?"

Fred told him, "It was Acts 2:42. I remember because I asked the pastor to give you the same verse I had. If you don't remember the words, I do. It goes like this: 'And they continued stedfastly in the apostles' doctrine and fellowship, and in breaking of bread, and in prayers.' This verse talks about the many people who were brought to faith in Christ on the day of Pentecost. It's very important that the Bible says they didn't just have one big religious day and then go their separate ways. They kept on listening to what the apostles taught them about the Lord Jesus. That kept them close to each other, too."

Ned was thoughtful. "Dad," he asked, "does that mean I have to go to church every Sunday for the rest of my life?"

His father answered, "Well, Ned, there are exceptions, you know. If you're sick, if there's some real emergency, if you have to travel, you may have to miss church. Pastor Martin even suggested that we might consider having a service some other time in the week for those who are often gone on weekends. The Bible doesn't say that it has to be on Sunday morning."

The youth suggested, "Maybe this chance to go fishing is an exception — you know, something special."

Fred said, "No, Son. It isn't. You can go fishing on Monday morning if you want to. And if you do go fishing with your friends on Sunday, you will be telling them that you don't care about hearing God's word any more than they do."

Ned asked, "You mean, I have to go to church, right?"

Fred said, "Not exactly. I don't want to force you to go to church. But I want to tell you how you should make the decision. You are a sinner. You have deserved to be punished by God for your sins. God the Son became a man and suffered all your punishment in your place on the cross. He died and rose again to forgive you all your sins. You learned about this from God's word. And you promised that you would hear his word faithfully all your life. Doesn't that just about sum it up?"

"Yes, Sir. I guess it does."

"Well, then, you do me a favor, OK? You think about that and then you tell me whether you're going to church tomorrow morning or not. Fair enough?"

18. The Man Who Worried About Church Finance

Read 1 John 3:13-18.

Pastor Martin, Fred, and the other officers of the congregation were at a meeting of the church council. The treasurer reported a sizeable deficit in the congregation's current expenses account. There was silence while the various officers tried to figure out something constructive to say. They talked about several plans for educating the congregation about the responsibilities of church membership. They finally decided to turn the matter over to the elders.

Pastor Martin added this comment and promise: "You all know that I don't like to preach about things like offerings to the church. Some people complain if they hear money mentioned in the sermon just once too often. But I guess I'm gonna have to include it in a sermon before too long." Several of the officers thought that was a very good idea.

Fred and a couple other officers stayed after the meeting to talk some more with Pastor Martin. One of them was saying, "Pastor, I know you always try to be a nice guy. I mean, that's part of your job. But you know, I really think you ought to lay it on the line about church finances."

"What do you mean?" asked the pastor.

The man replied, "I mean, no more pussyfooting. You know, tell people where it's at. Give them the facts and figures in your sermon. Tell them they have got to give more money to the church."

Somebody else chimed in, "That's right. Nothing else is free in this life. I wish the church could send out bills or something. Could we do that?"

Fred spoke up sarcastically, "That's a thought! Sending out bills for church membership sure means that all the people who never come would want their names taken off the membership list. That would solve one problem."

Pastor Martin interrupted that kind of thinking. "Lutheran churches don't send out bills. For one thing, how could we do it fairly? We don't know what everybody is earning. Would it be fair to charge a flat rate? No, it wouldn't. Just in earthly terms of fairness, it could not be done right. Besides, that isn't how God wants it done."

One of the men spoke up again, "But, Pastor, why do we have to go through this every year? Why do we have to worry about meeting our budget all the time?"

Pastor Martin answered, "We shouldn't really worry about it. We should just each do our best, act responsibly, make the best decisions in church council, too. We really have to leave the results up to God."

Fred said, "But, Pastor, that kind of thinking would never make it in the business world."

Pastor Martin responded, "Not many businessmen think that way, but even in business they really should. In the Psalms (127:1) it says, 'Except the Lord build the house, they labor in vain that built it.' "

"OK. You're right," Fred agreed, "but still, we have to deal with facts. When I wasn't an active church member, I used to think that the church would always be there when I needed it. But looking at these financial figures, I see that that isn't necessarily so. The church needs to be supported by its members."

Pastor Martin said, "That's true, in a way. But let's not leave God out of the picture."

The other man suggested, "Look, Pastor, maybe some of these things should be said by someone besides you. Maybe one of the elders should get up after the service some Sunday and talk turkey. Uh, there are a lot of things to be said. People have to be reminded that the church gets bills, you know. They need to be told that we have to pay your salary and your car allowance. We gotta pay utility bills and mortgage installments and all that stuff. And inflation hits the church, too."

Another man put in, "Yeah, and they need to be reminded that we have to pay bills over the summer, too. You know, people should see that they give money during vacation time, too."

"That's all true, and it's all important," Pastor Martin agreed. "Maybe it would be good for everybody to hear that again. I'm sure they have all heard it before. But people do need to be reminded of these things."

Fred said, "But there's something that worries me about that approach. For one thing, people need to be told that it isn't just their *money* that we're after. We want them to be active in other ways, too. It's not just money. It's contributing time and effort and ability, isn't it?"

Pastor Martin said, "That's true, too. People should be contributing their time and their abilities to the church in any number of ways. A lot of things can be done to help out. Whatever people have received is a gift from God, and they should use it to some extent for the spreading of God's word. There's lots to be done."

One of the men said, "But the problem now is finances."

Fred went on, "The other thing that is bugging me, though, is this: is it enough to tell people that we need money? Is that going to make them give more?"

101

Pastor Martin said, "Well, my experience is that telling people we need money will raise some money, but it won't solve the real problem. If we just tell people we need more money, well, to put it bluntly, the people who are already giving a lot will give even more. Most of the others will just find that another reason to complain. The real problem is how to motivate those who are giving a small portion of their income to give a larger proportion."

One of the men said, "Pastor, why don't we just set a specific figure. Why don't we say that every family should be giving, say, $30 a week? That would give everybody something to shoot for, wouldn't it?"

Pastor Martin said, "That wouldn't be fair, because not everybody is earning the same. The Bible says that free-will giving should be proportionate, based on how much one receives. Remember the widow who gave a very little bit of money, but it was all she had? Jesus praised her and said that she had given more than the rich people who gave much larger sums of money but did so without making a dent in their bank accounts, so to speak."

Fred came back to the point he had been trying to make: "Pastor, I get very impatient with people who don't give much to the church. I know I used to be one of them, but now I just don't understand that kind of thinking anymore. You've gotta preach a sermon on this that is gonna move people. Why don't you just tell them in so many words that Christians have to give to support the church?"

It was quiet for a moment when Fred said this so bluntly. Then Fred went on: "Wouldn't that be right, Pastor? Tell them that in order to be Christians they have to give money to support the church?"

Pastor Martin said, "No, that wouldn't be right. I don't think you realize what you are saying, Fred. Wouldn't that be telling people that they have to give money to get to heaven? Wouldn't that be works righteousness, trying to save themselves by the good works of giving money to support the church? At least, that's how a lot of people would understand it."

"Yeah, I guess you're right," Fred admitted, "but how else can we get people to give?"

Pastor Martin said, "Fred, I didn't mean to come down hard on you before. Pastors are tempted to talk to their people in the terms you suggested. I can remember a time or two when I've come close to saying those things. But it would be barking up the wrong tree. That would be using the law instead of the gospel.

"It's easy for us to think that we can move people to do things by using the law, but it doesn't really work that way. It would be like yelling at your kids and getting them to clean up their rooms at home by threatening. They might do it, but they would resent it, and they would be angry at you for it. We don't want people to resent giving money to the church. We want them to give willingly, gladly. The Bible says, 'God loveth a cheerful giver' " (2 Corinthians 9:7).

"So how do we do that?" Fred asked.

Pastor Martin said, "We don't do it. God does it through his word. For instance, I can see it in the Epistle for this coming Sunday. It's in 1 John, chapter 3. There's a lot in that chapter, and I was thinking about several good points I could show people in that text. But I could talk about stewardship, too. Listen to verse 16." Pastor Martin took out his pocket New Testament and read: "Hereby perceive we the love of God, because he laid down his life for us: and we ought to lay down our lives for the brethren."

Pastor Martin explained: "God does not love us because we are good. He loves us because he is good. He loves us so much that, even though we were nothing but sinners, still the Father sent the Son, and the Son went willingly to the cross. He suffered and died for the forgiveness of all our sins. Jesus himself said, 'Greater love hath no man than this, that a man lay down his life for his friends' (John 15:13).

"Jesus didn't just talk about it. He did it, for us. He died to pay the penalty for all our sins. That's the gospel, and it is the gospel that should move us to all kinds of wonderful good works, including offering freely and willingly, offering money and time and effort to support the preaching of the word and to spread that word around the world.

"Here God says that Christians should be willing, if necessary, even to lay down their lives for the sake of their fellow Christians. That would be the greatest sacrifice anyone could make. If we are willing to do that much, then we are certainly willing to do all kinds of lesser things, like giving just a portion of our income so that there is a building where the word of God is preached and taught — and so that there is a full-time pastor who can preach and teach it, instruct the young, etc. So, you see, Christians don't give because they have to. They give because they want to."

Fred said, "I remember hearing that before, right after I got to be active again in the church. But it's hard to keep on thinking that way. It is a powerful reason to give, though."

Pastor Martin said, "Sure, it's hard to keep on thinking that way. It's hard to keep the gospel in mind, and all of us naturally tend to think in terms of the law. That's why we need to keep hearing the gospel — and that's why, Sunday, when I preach about stewardship and giving, I'll try very hard to keep it clearly in terms of the gospel of God's love, grace, forgiveness, and salvation in Christ."

19. The Man Who Worried About Faith

Read Isaiah 44:21-23.

There was a time in Fred's life when he got into some severe spiritual trials. He did not get into trouble by doing something or getting involved in something that seemed bad, evil, wicked, or otherwise spiritually unhealthy. He got into trouble by doing some things that seemed like the best things for a Christian to do.

It started with Fred's hunger for the word of God. There is nothing wrong with that. Fred and his family were reading the Bible at home and were using it in family devotions. The children went to Sunday school and the parents went to Bible class. So far, so good.

But then Fred got the idea that he wanted something more. He did not know what it was that he wanted. It was just something more, something different. So he started looking around.

Pastor Martin suggested some good books for Fred to read. But Fred was not satisfied with them. So he started to watch all kinds of religious programs on television. He listened to a religious radio station in the car. He bought some books that were displayed very attractively in a local shop. He was searching again in the spiritual realm. He was not satisfied. Somehow he had the vague feeling that he was missing something.

Fred was acting like a hunting dog that has lost the scent. It casts about here and there sniffing at just about anything and everything, hoping somehow to find the scent again. Now dogs are not very particular about what they stick their noses into. Neither was Fred.

But Fred did not find satisfaction or peace. He was getting more disturbed. It was not that he did not understand what he was hearing and reading from these non-Lutheran sources. Rather, he did understand it. He understood it very well. He understood it almost too well. It was a lot easier to understand than what he thought he was hearing from Pastor Martin.

Fred thought he was growing, maturing, making progress in spiritual matters. But that did not make him happy. He thought that he had found the way to make sense out of the biblical message. But that did not make him content. He thought he understood a few things better than Pastor Martin. Maybe if he went and showed them to the pastor and convinced him about them, then things would fall into place.

So Fred made an appointment to meet Pastor Martin in his study on a Saturday morning. Pastor Martin was already there, doing this and that, when Fred arrived. He greeted Fred and offered him a comfortable chair in his study. They sat and chatted a while. Then Pastor Martin said, "Fred, I don't mind chatting, not at all. But I did get the impression that you had something specific you wanted to talk over."

Fred said, "That's true, Pastor. I've been doing some reading and some studying, and I wanted to talk to you about some of the things I've found out."

Pastor Martin figured that he should go slowly. He asked, "What have you been reading?"

Fred opened his briefcase and showed Pastor Martin some of the books. They were by well-known religious figures. One was by a television evangelist and had a title suggesting that it could unlock some mysteries or secrets that had previously not been understood. Another was by a famous preacher, and its title suggested that it laid out a simple method by which a person could make himself a believer in Christ. A third book proclaimed from its brightly colored cover that religious decisions were up to the individual.

Pastor Martin took the books and looked at the glowing praise of the authors that was printed on the back covers. He opened them and read the table of contents in each one. He noted that these books contained chapters proclaiming the individual's spiritual free will. They emphasized a person's supposed ability to make himself a believer in Christ. They made faith out to be a human work that appeased God. Pastor Martin handed the books back to Fred without saying anything.

Fred asked him, "What do you think? Have you ever read these books?"

Pastor Martin said, "I read one of them a few years ago. The others I haven't seen before. But I think I know what's in them. I mean, it is well known what these writers stand for, what kind of teachings they promote."

Fred pursued the matter, "But I think maybe you should read them. They could help you with your sermons. There are some things in there that are more clearly said than you say them."

"Like what?"

"Well, they talk a lot more about faith than you do."

"What do they say about faith?" He thought he knew, but he was interested in what Fred understood them to be saying.

Fred said, "Well, they emphasize that you've gotta believe in order to have your sins forgiven. You always make it out that our sins are forgiven because Jesus died on the cross. But these books have shown me that our sins are forgiven because we believe. We've gotta accept it. You know, God has done his part, and that is well and good. But there is still something left for us to do, and that is to believe, to accept it. We have to trust God and then he will forgive us. But there is no forgiveness before that time."

Pastor Martin asked, "Fred, did you ever just decide to believe anything?"

"What do you mean?"

"I mean, why do you believe that the sun is shining brightly?" He gestured out the window.

"Why, I believe it because I see it."

"Did you decide to believe it or do you believe it because the sunshine makes a pretty strong impression on the old eyes?"

"Well, I guess I believe it because the sun is pretty bright."

Pastor Martin continued, "Right. We believe that the sun is shining or the rain is falling because something outside of us convinces us that it is true. Somebody who can decide to believe what he wants to about the weather has got problems. That's all I can say. Faith in Christ is like seeing the light. We didn't decide to have eyes. God gave them to us. We didn't decide to have faith. God gave it to us through his word, a word that comes from outside us."

Fred looked unconvinced. Pastor Martin went on, "Your faith doesn't make God forgive you any more than your eyes make the sun shine. Your eyes receive the light that is coming down anyway. Your faith receives the forgiveness of sins that Christ has already earned. And your faith, like your eyes, is a creation of God."

"That's hard to understand," Fred objected.

The pastor explained, "If our faith were just something inside of us, just something we decided to believe, then it wouldn't be true. It would just be wishful thinking."

"But don't we have free will?" Fred asked.

"We don't have free will in spiritual matters," the pastor explained. "We can't decide to believe in Jesus. The Bible says we can't even know anything about spiritual matters without the Holy Spirit. In 2 Corinthians 2:14 it says. . . . "

Fred objected, "But if ony believers are saved, then it must be our faith and not Jesus' death that makes God forgive our sins."

Fred and the pastor went around and around for a while. The pastor tried to show Fred, in fact, did show him with several different Bible verses that faith is itself a gift from God, the gift that receives forgiveness. But forgiveness is based only on the work of Christ.

Fred kept talking about his new understanding of the need for a personal, individual decision to believe in Christ. Only that, he said, could make God stop being angry. The pastor kept showing him from the Bible that man cannot decide to believe in Christ by his own free will but that the Holy Spirit produces faith by means of the powerful gospel message. Fred insisted on free will.

The pastor remained calm although he was getting frustrated. Fred got a bit hot under the collar. Pastor Martin decided that it was time to cut the discussion short because it was producing more heat than light. Fred left in a friendly enough way. They agreed to talk about it again another time. Each agreed to think about what the other had said. But Pastor Martin's last comment was, "Fred, I think you need to ask yourself if you might not have started thinking this way because of human reason, not because of the word of God. And I wonder if it has given you peace with God or if it has made you less confident, less trusting, less peaceful. That's what I wonder."

Fred went out and got into his car. As he drove off, he tuned in the religious radio station that he had been listening to lately. It was broadcasting a sermon by a famous preacher, whose voice Fred recognized instantly. The voice was saying, "And so, my friends, if you want the forgiveness of sins, if you want Christ living in your life, if you want to be right with God, then you, you, you have to make the free-will decision to let Christ into your life. Nobody's gonna help you. God's not gonna help you. It's up to you. God makes you a really good offer. It's up to you to take him up on it."

Fred angrily switched the radio off. For some reason, it was clear to him why he had been trying to convince Pastor Martin of his new position. It made sense to his human mind, but it did not give him peace. He had imagined that if the pastor agreed with him, then the pastor would still find some way to help him find comfort in it. Why had he started believing this new way? Was it because of the Bible? No, it was because it had made sense to his mind, and because it had appealed to him to be able to take some of the credit for salvation. It had made him proud.

The problem was, to put it bluntly, that if God did not even help a person to be converted, then everything really depended on that person's own strength. In fact, Fred realized, if salvation depended at all on a person's own contribution, if anything necessary to salvation had to be man's own doing, then salvation did depend on man. These preachers were telling people to trust themselves, not God! Fred did not feel very trustworthy just then.

He turned the corner very quickly and went around the block. He parked back at the church and went in. A bit sheepishly he knocked on the door of the pastor's study. He found the pastor sitting at his desk with his Bible open. That already told Fred something.

Fred said, "Uh, Pastor, I guess it didn't take me too long to get to wondering about what you said. I'm sorry for upsetting you before."

"That's OK." Pastor Martin interjected.

Fred continued, "But I got into the car and tuned in a sermon on the radio and heard somebody else saying what I had been saying. Suddenly it all made sense to me, I mean, what you were saying. I realized that I had been proud and was using my mind instead of really reading the Bible on its own terms. I realized that I was proud and wanted to take some of the credit for my own salvation. And I realized that if I had to count on myself for salvation, I could not be sure of being saved. Is that what you were trying to tell me?"

Pastor Martin said, "Yes, that is what was wrong with the way you were thinking. You see, those books you showed me and the things you've been listening to make some big mistakes. The key thing is that they make faith a good work. When they talk about being saved by faith, it sounds like what the Bible says. But the difference is that they make faith a good work that appeases God's anger. So, although they talk about salvation by faith, they really push salvation by works. It's just that, for them, faith becomes the main good work. They are looking to themselves instead of looking to God for salvation."

"I see that now," Fred admitted. "The problem is that now I'm confused about how we get saved."

The pastor put his hand on Fred's shoulder and said, "Fred, pull that chair up to the desk and let's look at something the Bible says."

Fred pulled up the chair as the pastor moved the Bible over to the corner of the desk so that they could both see it.

Pastor Martin said, "Now I just love the Book of Isaiah, and after our discussion I turned to it to reread some of my favorite passages. I was just thinking that I wanted to show you these verses in Isaiah 44. God says to his people, 'Remember these, O Jacob and Israel; for thou art my servant: I have formed thee; thou art my servant: O Israel, thou shalt not be forgotten of me.'

"Here God tells the people to remember something because it is very important. It is God who has made us his servants. We do not become God's servants by applying for the position or deciding to take it up. No, God chooses us.

"Then the next verse says, 'I have blotted out, as a thick cloud, thy transgressions, and, as a cloud, thy sins: return unto me; for I have redeemed thee.' Our sins came between us and God just as clouds come between the earth and the sun in the sky. But how do those clouds get taken out of the way? The earth doesn't do it. The sun burns away the cloud cover or the sun warms the air and causes winds that blow the clouds away.

"That's the way it is with salvation. God has removed the sins that were between us and him. He redeemed us by the blood of his Son, our Lord, Jesus Christ. He has taken away the darkness and again shines on us. His anger is removed and his grace shines on us like the sun.

"That's why, when it says to remember or to return to God, it is not spelling out what we need to do to make God love us. Nothing of the kind. It is based on all that God has already done for us in Christ.

"That's why the next verse says, 'Sing, O ye heavens; for the Lord hath done it: shout, ye lower parts of the earth: break forth into singing, ye mountains, O forest, and every tree therein: for the Lord hath redeemed Jacob, and glorified himself in Israel.' See how it says that God did it? He has glorified himself in saving us and in making us his people."

Fred said, "Thanks, Pastor. I guess we have to stay with what the Bible says. That's where real comfort and peace are given to us."

20. The Man Who Worried About Damnation

Read Isaiah 65:1,2.

Fred had gotten into a very dangerous way of thinking. He had been led — or misled — into believing that a person must make himself a believer in Christ. This idea had appealed to his human pride, but it had also worried him when he remembered his human weakness and the conflicts, doubts, and problems that continued to plague him in his Christian life.

Pastor Martin had used some passages from the book of Isaiah to show Fred that salvation is entirely dependent on God. God had redeemed us, paying the price for our sins by the death of the God-Man Jesus Christ. The Father sent the Son to die for us. Then the Father and the Son together sent the Holy Spirit to convert us, that is, to bring us to faith and to keep us in the faith. Fred learned that God gets the credit — all the credit — for salvation. This was important for him to know. He was to rely and depend on God, not on himself.

Needless to say, Fred wanted to share this information with his wife Leona. She had been interested in his new line of thinking, but she had never accepted it completely. She was actually quite relieved to learn that Fred had been brought back to his former opinion. They talked about it, studied the Bible together, and were strengthened in the faith in which they had been instructed.

But Leona still had a big question. It was something she had never really asked herself before. She said, "Fred, I'm puzzled about the other side of the coin."

"What do you mean?"

"We see that the Bible gives God the credit for our salvation, and that is a comforting, reassuring thought for us. We don't have to rely on ourselves."

"Right!"

"How about the people who go to hell? Why aren't they saved? Why aren't they converted? Doesn't God want to save them? Or can't he save them?"

"I guess he can if he wants to, but I have always thought that God wanted every one to be saved."

"That's what I'm asking about. Didn't it occur to you to ask the pastor about that?"

"No, it didn't," Fred admitted. "Wait a minute. Let's not get upset. We've never asked this question before. It may take a while to get to the answer. Look, we can't *blame* God for people getting damned. I mean, we can't *blame* God for anything, can we?"

"No, I don't think we can or should blame God for anything," Leona agreed. "I didn't mean to say that God is to blame for people going to hell. I'm just asking 'Why?' "

"If God can save them, and if only God can save them, and if God wants to save them, why aren't they saved?" Fred asked.

"That's what I'm asking," Leona repeated.

"Well, I just want to be sure we understand the question."

"It's more important to understand the answer."

114

"But we don't know the answer."

Fred sat there thinking about it. Leona sat there thinking about it. The Bible was on the table between them. They each thought about opening it to look for the answer, but they did not know where to look.

Finally Fred said, "Look. Let's not get into any kind of problem with this. I'm going to phone the pastor and find out if he can give us some kind of simple answer."

Fred phoned the church. Pastor Martin was still there and answered the phone. Quickly Fred outlined the question they had been discussing. Then he asked, "Pastor, can you give us some kind of simple, straightforward answer?"

Pastor Martin said, "This is a good question. Look, I'm on my way out now, and I could stop by for a few minutes at your place and try to give you an answer."

Fred agreed. Since they did not live very far from the church, the pastor was there in about ten minutes. Leona was still thinking it over while she made coffee. But Fred had picked up the Saturday paper and was reading the comics.

After the usual pleasantries, as they were sitting in the living room with their coffee, they discussed the question at issue. Pastor Martin began, "I remember taking a course in Christian history at the seminary. The professor said that this question was one of the most perplexing in the history of theology. There were people on each side of it. Some people have said that man gets the blame for his damnation if he is damned. But they usually also say that man gets some of the credit for his own salvation if he is saved. That would seem to be logical."

Fred interrupted, "But we already saw this morning from the Bible that God gets all the credit for salvation. So that option is out."

"Right," said the pastor. "I guess I'm remembering that professor of mine. You know how professors love to give long answers. Anyway, the other option is basically with those who give God the credit for salvation, but they also

115

give him the blame for damnation. Only they usually say that they are giving him the credit for damnation because damnation and hell are also for God's glory. Don't ask me how they can be comfortable with that kind of thinking. I certainly don't want that kind of God for my God — and that is not the God of the Bible."

"That's horrible. Why would anybody think that way?" Leona asked.

"It's logical, and man's mind is proud," the pastor replied. "You see, either of those answers makes sense. It makes sense to make both salvation and damnation depend either on man or on God. That makes sense to the human mind. But it isn't what the Bible teaches."

"What does the Bible teach?" Fred asked.

"Quite simply, the Bible gives man the blame for damnation and God the credit for salvation," the pastor replied. "Man gets himself damned. God gets us saved."

"Can you show me that in the Bible?" Fred asked.

"Very easily," said the pastor. He picked up their Bible from the table and opened it to Acts 13. He showed them verse 46, where Paul and Barnabas said to some people who were Jews but who had not believed the gospel when they heard it, "It was necessary that the word of God should first have been spoken to you: but seeing ye put it from you, and judge yourselves unworthy of everlasting life, lo, we turn to the Gentiles."

The pastor commented, "See, these people were not believers and did not become believers and so were not saved. Why? Because they rejected the word of God. This verse is very literally translated here. They put it away from them. They pushed it away. They rejected it. They get the blame. Remember, the New Testament also says that God 'will have all men to be saved, and to come unto the knowledge of the truth' " (1 Timothy 2:4).

Then the pastor went down to verse 48 in Acts 13 and read, "And when the Gentiles heard this, they were glad,

116

and glorified the word of the Lord: and as many as were ordained to eternal life believed."

Pastor Martin commented, "Here these people became believers. God had arranged it that way. He had chosen and ordained them to eternal life."

Fred summed the matter up, "So the facts are really pretty simple. God wants to save everybody. Those who are saved owe their salvation entirely to him. But those who are damned have nobody to blame but themselves."

"Right," said the pastor.

"Wait a minute," said Leona. "This is all well and good, and I see what the Bible is saying. But it still doesn't answer the question. I want to know why some people are saved and some people are damned."

"Yeah, I see that, too," Fred chimed in. "Pastor, you showed us the facts in the Bible. But you didn't show us where the Bible says why it is that way."

Pastor Martin explained, "The reason I didn't show you where the Bible answers the question is that the Bible doesn't answer the question. It just doesn't tell us why."

"You mean in that whole big book it never once says why some are saved and some are damned?" Leona asked.

Pastor Martin said, "That's right. I remember a detective show I used to watch on television when I was a kid. Every time this detective interviewed a witness, he said he just wanted the facts. That's how it is here. We have the facts, but we don't have the explanation. Just as the Bible does not explain the Trinity, or how God became man in Christ, so it does not explain why some are saved and some are damned."

Fred and Leona sat there quietly for a couple of minutes. Then Pastor Martin went on, "We shouldn't feel bad about not being able to know why some are saved and some are damned. God has not seen fit to reveal it to us. Even the Apostle Paul was stopped short here. When he dealt with it, all he could do was what I did before, Fred, namely, to quote the Bible. In fact, let me show you."

117

He opened the Bible to Romans 10 and showed them the last two verses: "But Esaias is very bold, and saith, I was found of them that sought me not; I was made manifest unto them that asked not after me. But to Israel he saith, All day long I have stretched forth my hands unto a disobedient and gainsaying people."

The pastor explained, "So Paul points to how Isaiah prophesied the same thing that Paul had experienced as we read in Acts, namely, that some people have the Bible and hear about Jesus over and over again and still are not converted. And it is their own fault that they have stayed with their unbelief, their rejection of God's word.

"But some people are converted by the word. People may be converted the one hundredth or the one thousandth time they hear the word. Or they may be converted the very first time. Or they may always resist and reject it. We don't know why. We cannot and must not try to answer for God. If he has not answered our question in the Bible, then we just have to leave it at that. We can ask the question, but we have to realize that we don't have the answer."

Fred said, "OK. We don't have the answer to this one. So what kind of attitude should we have?"

Pastor Martin said, "As in everything else, we should trust God. He wants everybody saved. Christ died on the cross for all the sins of the whole world. He did enough for everybody who ever has lived, lives now, or ever will live. The Holy Ghost has converted you through baptism and the word, and it's the Holy Ghost's job to keep you a Christian through the word and the sacrament. He wants to do it. He will do it."

"So really, even though we can't answer all the questions, that shouldn't make us sad," Leona observed.

"Right," said Fred. "It doesn't change anything."

"The chief purpose of the Bible is still the same" Pastor Martin reminded them. "It was written to give us faith and to strengthen our faith in Christ. It is to give us a joyful hope for salvation, a hope that depends and relies on God, not on ourselves. And that hope will not be disappointed."

21. The Man Who Worried About Difficulty

Read John 12:23-26.

Fred's friend Sam had gotten married. It happened like this: One evening, while visting Fred and Leona, he had met a distant cousin of Leona's. Her name was Sharon. It was one of those so-called whirlwind romances. They were married after knowing each other only a matter of months. Before marrying, they were sure that they understood what family and friends and the pastor were telling them about the effort and energy that they would have to put into marriage. But it is questionable whether anyone really understands that before being married.

At first everything had gone so well. Sam and Sharon often visited Fred and Leona. Everything seemed fine and happy. Then after several months Fred and Leona were not getting together as much with Sam and Sharon. Leona was a bit worried, but Fred said that it was just because everyone had so many things to do. Fred was not quite right.

One Friday evening about ten o'clock, Fred and Leona heard a knock on the door. Fred went to the door and found Sam there with a suitcase in his hand.

Fred said, "Uh, hi, Sam. Come on in. What's up?"

Sam stepped inside the door and set his suitcase down. He said, "Thanks, Fred. I need a place to stay for a few days. I thought maybe I could sack out on your couch."

Fred said, "Well, I suppose so. But, uh, what about Sharon? I mean, maybe we could have some kind of explanation?"

Fred said a word to Leona, who had just made some coffee. She promised to pour some for the three of them. Fred took Sam into the den where there was a couch he could sleep on and have some privacy.

When they were all seated, coffee cups in hand, Leona said, "So, Sam, why don't you tell us what's wrong?"

"Probably just a little lovers' spat, right?" suggested Fred hopefully.

"No, Fred," said Sam. "It's a lot more serious than that. I've left Sharon for good, and I just want to camp out here if it's OK until I find a new apartment."

Leona said, "That's terrible. You talk as if there were no hope of getting back together with Sharon."

"I'm afraid there isn't any hope," said Sam. "My mind's made up."

They talked things over, and the explanation that came out was unfortunately all too common. It was really a matter of everyday frictions and irritations that had mushroomed into frequent quarreling. Finally Sam had decided he wanted out of the marriage. Sharon still wanted to try to work things out, but Sam insisted on calling it quits.

After they had heard the story, Fred and Leona exchanged glances. Fred took a deep breath and said, "But Sam, you know that Jesus said that adultery is the only legitimate reason for divorce. You haven't got grounds for divorce. You promised to stay with Sharon as long as you both live."

Sam said, "Yeah, well, I've done a lot of thinking lately, and I don't know if that really applies anymore. I mean, times have changed. Besides, I've been praying about this."

Fred said, "Come on, Sam! Prayer is you talking to God. But God talks to you in the Bible. So how can prayer tell you what's right? God's word tells us what's right and wrong."

"Don't confuse me with the Bible right now," Sam objected. "I know what I'm doing."

About that time they agreed that it was time to call it a day. Fred fetched some blankets for Sam while Leona quietly phoned Sharon to make sure that she was all right and to offer any possible help. Sharon was upset but remained sensible enough not to do anything rash or hasty. She knew that the best thing just then was to give her husband a little time. Leona promised to call again the next day.

Fred did not sleep much that night. So the next morning, before Sam was up, Fred phoned the parsonage. Pastor Martin agreed to meet Fred in a quiet restaurant for a little breakfast. Once they were there, Fred quickly gave Pastor Martin the basic facts. By the time their food arrived, Fred was asking, "What do you think, Pastor?"

Pastor Martin replied, "I think that Sam and Sharon should have talked it over with me months ago. But that's the way it usually is. People don't call the pastor about marital problems until things have gotten pretty serious."

"Well, OK," said Fred. "But the question is: what are we gonna do now?"

"Right," said Pastor Martin. "You were certainly correct when you told Sam that it is his duty to Sharon — and to God — to stay with Sharon and work things out. That is the committment that God expects — that he demands in marriage. No matter how unhappy you may be, that is not any reason to take a powder. It's a lifelong committment — for better or worse."

"I told Sam that," said Fred, "but it didn't seem to change his mind. He just sort of started getting angry. So I didn't push it."

Pastor Martin said, "This is a matter of God's law. When people don't want to obey the law — and don't want to be reminded of their obligations — it often does make them angry."

"Sam has quite a temper," Fred told the pastor. "I know because I've seen it. He can be very unpleasant — in fact, downright ugly."

Pastor Martin said, "That puts you and me in a position similar to his."

"What do you mean?" asked Fred.

The pastor told him, "I am his pastor, and you are his brother in Christ. We have the difficult job of telling him he's going against God's expressed will. We have to face this task whether we want to or not, no matter how angry he might get."

"Yeah," said Fred. "I get it. He has a responsibility to Sharon. We have a responsibility to him. It's not the same as marriage, but it is a responsibility."

"But it's not all that bleak," Pastor Martin reassured Fred. "In both cases there is hope. There is hope that Sam will repent for leaving Sharon, and there is hope that they can make a new start as husband and wife."

Fred said, "It's still hard to face up to difficulties, especially when so many people are running away from them these days."

"But as Christians," said Pastor Martin, "we have before us the best example of someone who did his duty no matter what the cost."

"Who?" asked Fred. Then he said, "Oh, yeah."

Pastor Martin opened his New Testament and read where Jesus said, "The hour is come, that the Son of man should be glorified. Verily, verily, I say unto you, Except a corn of wheat fall into the ground and die, it abideth alone: but if it die, it bringeth forth much fruit."

The pastor explained, "Jesus said those words not many days before he was crucified. He was glorified by going the way of the cross. He faced a lot more grief, pain, sorrow, and suffering than we will ever face. And he went to it bravely anyway — because that was the will of his Father and because that was the only way for us to be saved."

"Right," said Fred. "If he hadn't died and risen again, our sins would not be forgiven."

The pastor went on, "The crucial thing is that he did die and rise again. He has paid the price for all our sins. Our sins are forgiven, and we do have eternal life."

Fred asked, "But now we still have some difficult duties in this life. Does what Jesus did help us there?"

"Sure," said Pastor Martin. "It helps us in two ways. First, I'm never tired of quoting 1 John 4:19, 'We love him, because he first loved us.' Christ's love for us in saving us from our sins moves us to love him more and more. And out of this love we begin again and again to do a better job of keeping the commandments."

Fred said, "That's what you call 'gospel motivation,' isn't it?"

"Yes," said the pastor. "Then, too, we have Jesus' example. He has shown us that much good comes from doing one's duty in spite of the difficulties and the unpleasantness that we may have to face."

Fred said, "So with this perspective, we shouldn't just tell Sam what to do but we should encourage him — I mean, we really have something to say that should encourage him."

The pastor said, "If the law moves him to repent, and the gospel stirs up his faith again, then he will be very strongly motivated to live his life the way Jesus wants him to. If he refuses to listen to God's word . . . " Here the pastor paused.

Fred interjected, "It could be serious."

The pastor said, "It could be critical, a real spiritual crossroad. Jesus also said, 'He that loveth his life shall lose it; and he that hateth his life in this world shall keep it unto life eternal.' "

"What does that mean?" asked Fred.

"It means," said Pastor Martin, "that if Sam tries to get earthly happiness by going against God's will, he is in real danger of losing his eternal salvation. But if, moved by God's word, he accepts the cross that God lays on him, eternal happiness is in store for him."

Fred objected, "But that sounds like earning one's way to heaven!"

The pastor explained further, "No, Christ's works have earned forgiveness and salvation. Our works do not. But what we are talking about here is simply that a person who truly believes in Jesus tries to do his will. But a person who consciously chooses a sinful way of life, that person has fallen away from the faith. He has lost his salvation — unless he is brought back to faith. David and Peter both fell away and were brought back, for example, David after committing adultery and murder, Peter after denying that he knew the Lord."

"There's a lot of comfort in what you are saying," Fred agreed, "but I am still bothered by something. Do you mean to imply that marriage is a matter of bearing the cross?"

Pastor Martin explained, "Some marriages are happier than others. Some are unhappier than others. But all married people face problems. If the Christian, for Jesus' sake, accepts the burden of responsibility and deals with the problems and bears up under what cannot be changed, then that is part of bearing the cross for Jesus' sake. That is especially true when the world makes it seem so easy, so blameless, even so natural to get a divorce."

Fred said, "So there are problems, but there is always hope, too."

The pastor said, "Right, but the Christian's main hope is not for this life but for the next life. There is hope and help for Sam in God's word, and there is hope and help for us, too. So maybe we had better go talk to Sam."

"How about another cup of coffee first?" Fred suggested.

"That won't make it any easier to confront Sam, will it?" asked Pastor Martin.

Fred paid the check and they left the restaurant.

124

 **22.** The Man Who Worried
About Belief

Read Mark 9:17-29.

Fred was home from work early one day, sitting in the
living room where the late afternoon sun gave him just the
right light by which to read the newspaper. He glanced out
the window in time to see his teenaged son Ned coming
home from school. He was engaged in a heated discussion
with one of his friends as they walked down the sidewalk.
They stood in front of the house for some minutes arguing.
But since it was a cold day, and the windows were closed,
Fred did not hear what they were talking about.

Ned stalked into the house, threw his books down on the
table, and hung up his jacket in the closet with more noise
than necessary. He came into the living room and flopped
down on the couch. Only then did he see his father sitting
in the chair by the window. Ned said, "Oh, hi, Dad! I didn't
know you were home."

"Hello, Son. What's wrong?"

"Oh, nothing."

"Come on, something's wrong. You can tell your dear old dad."

"Really, Dad. There's nothing wrong with me. It's just that dumb school and all the people in it."

His father asked, "So what went wrong today?"

Ned told him, "Oh, its the same old stuff. You know. I've got this biology class the last period. And they're always talking about evolution."

So Fred asked, "And that bothers you quite a bit?"

"Well," said the son, "it's getting to me. I try to argue back. That's what we were arguing about in front of the house — in fact, all the way home."

Fred asked his son, "Did you ever convince anybody by arguing about it?"

Ned replied, "No. I never did. I try real hard, but nobody listens. Uh, Dad, it doesn't help to get angry about it, does it?"

"No, Son," said Fred. "It doesn't help. When you get angry trying to prove a point, it just makes other people get angry, too. Or else it makes them wonder if you have any good reason to believe what you say. They think you're getting angry because you're afraid of losing the argument."

Ned asked, "Dad, do we have a real good reason to believe what theBible says about six-day creation? I mean, the pastor made a big deal out of it in confirmation class, and I guess the Bible doesn't leave any room for belief in evolution. But how important is it?"

"Well, that's two questions," Fred replied, "and I guess the answer's the same for both of them. God says it in the Bible. Since he says so, that makes it so. I mean, he was the only witness to creation, right? And his word makes it important for us to believe."

The boy said, "Still, sometimes, it's kind of hard. I mean, they've got all these fossils and stuff. I want to believe what the Bible says, but sometimes I don't know."

126

Fred promised his son, "I'll call Pastor Martin. He said once that he had some books that show that believing in creation can be supported by scientific evidence, too, not just by the Bible."

Fred phoned the pastor, who suggested that Fred come over to see him. There was still plenty of time before dinner, so Fred drove over to the parsonage where the pastor was at work in his study. He sat down in the chair the pastor offered him.

Pastor Martin asked, "So what's this about creation and evolution?"

Fred explained his son's difficulties with his teacher and his classmates.

The pastor said, "Now I certainly can show you some books I have read on this topic. You're welcome to borrow them for as long as you need them." He searched his shelves until he found the two books he was thinking of. Fred took them, thanked the pastor and started leafing through them.

Then Pastor Martin said, "There is another problem here, though."

"What's that?"

"The problem is one of faith against unbelief."

"Do you think my boy is in danger of falling away from the Christian faith?"

Pastor Martin reassured him, "No, it's not that. I just mean that he — like just about all Christians — has doubts sometimes about God's word. The scientific evidence in those books is not really going to answer the questions about his faith in God's word. Our faith must stand only on God's word — only in God's power. So I don't suspect that Ned is falling away from the faith — just that his faith is being tried. But if you think your son is in danger of losing his faith, you might want to discuss that with him — or ask him to talk to me about it."

Fred considered, "I don't know. There might be something in what you say."

Pastor Martin picked up, "There are scientific arguments with real, hard, factual evidence for creation, but our faith must not rest on them. The Epistle to the Hebrews says, 'Through faith we understand that the worlds were framed by the word of God, so that things which are seen were not made of things which do appear' (Hebrews 11:3). Even though there are scientific proofs, we believe what the Bible says — with or without them, for or against the current trends in worldly thinking."

"So maybe I shouldn't show him these books after all?" Fred wondered.

The pastor answered, "No, I'm not saying that. Show him the books. But just make clear to him that the real reason for believing in creation is not science but the word of God."

Fred coughed and looked a bit embarassed. "Pastor," he said, "I have to admit that I sometimes have doubts, too."

The pastor said, "So do I."

Fred looked surprised.

"Hey, I'm a sinner, just like you," the pastor said, "and unbelief is a sin. And I am tempted to sin just as much as anyone else. I'm not perfect. I wish I were — and I look forward to being perfect in heaven. But here and now, well, I have doubts at times, too."

"I never thought of that, Pastor. How do you deal with your doubts?" Fred asked.

The pastor said, "Whenever Satan attacks me with doubt, I just go back to the Bible. I read or think about what the Bible says. God's power is behind that word and in it and with it — and God works through it to convince us of its truth."

Fred said thoughtfully, "There are so many areas where the modern world tells us that that Bible is wrong. I was just reading the newspaper before Ned came home. There was some columnist saying that anything sexual is all right, no matter what any religious authority says. And just the other week in the religion section they even had some Rev.

Somebody-or-Other writing that Jesus' miracles did not really happen. He claimed they were all just legends made up by people who thought Jesus was really great."

Pastor Martin said, "You know, the Bible is the best seller. More copies of the Bible are sold each year than of any other book in the world. But people say it's read less than any other book. The most bought and the least read book."

"I believe that," said Fred. "I know a lot of people who have Bibles in their homes gathering dust."

Pastor Martin went on, "And a lot of those who do read the Bible, don't believe it."

"Why is that?" asked Fred. "I mean, I have doubts, but that's only sometimes. Of course, I was raised with the Bible."

The pastor said, "But faith, real faith in Christ, is a gift from God. It is not something we can produce in ourselves. We who have faith give God the credit for giving it to us through his word and baptism. It's like the man in the ninth chapter of Mark who brought his son to have Jesus cast a demon out of him. The man had faith in Christ to cast out the demon, but he also doubted. So when he asked Jesus to do the miracle, he also put in 'if thou canst.' That shows that he also had some doubt.

"Jesus turned it back on him and said, 'If thou canst believe, all things are possible to him that believeth.' The man showed then that he had also learned where to have his faith strengthened against doubt. He said to Jesus, 'Lord, I believe; help thou mine unbelief.' "

Fred said, "So to have his faith strengthened he turned to God, who had given him the faith in the first place."

"Right," said the pastor. "God gives us faith and God is the one who must strengthen that faith. He does strengthen our faith in him through the word and the Lord's Supper."

Fred concluded, "So if we have trouble with something like, say, creation, the thing to do is to pray to God to strengthen our faith and then to read the Bible."

"Exactly," said the pastor. "But there is something much harder to believe than six-day creation, much harder to believe than all the miracles reported in the Bible, much harder to believe than the way the Bible goes against today's standards of morality — or, I should say, immorality. There is something that is so impossible to believe that we need to read what the Bible says about it over and over again. We need to hear it preached about every Sunday."

"What's that?"

"The gospel."

"What do you mean?"

The pastor said, "I mean that we are sinners. We know that we are sinners. If we are honest with ourselves, honest about the way we are in our hearts, then we know that we are sinners and have deserved only to be punished by God — here and in hell.

"Our consciences, the world, the word of law in the Bible all condemn us. Our hearts become afraid. That is the worst and most dangerous and most difficult kind of doubt — when we doubt that our sins are forgiven, when we doubt that God is gracious to us, when we doubt that we have eternal life and salvation for Jesus' sake."

"I see what you mean," said Fred.

The pastor went on, "That's the real tough point. For us to believe by our own reasoning or effort that God has actually condemned his Son Jesus Christ to death on the cross for our sins, in our place — that is the hardest thing in the Bible to believe. And by *believe*, we do not mean simply to accept it as a fact but actually to trust God, to trust that he has forgiven our sins for Jesus' sake. Now he has forgiven our sins — and that is the main point of the whole Bible. But how are we to believe it when we know what sinners we are?"

Fred said, "That's when we have to go back to the fact that Luther pointed to in the *Small Catechism*, that we can't believe on our own but the Holy Ghost has brought us to faith."

130

The pastor picked up on the thought, "That's exactly it. The Bible says, 'The natural man receiveth not the things of the Spirit of God: for they are foolishness unto him: neither can he know them, for they are spiritually discerned' " (1 Corinthians 2:14).

After a pause, the pastor said, "So, after all, we are very much like that man in the Bible who said to Jesus, 'Lord, I believe; help thou mine unbelief.' We have our doubts. We pray to Jesus to strengthen our faith. But then we shouldn't just sit around and wait for him to do something. We should open the Bible and read it. We should go to church and hear his word preached and taught. We have the promise that the Holy Spirit will keep us in the faith to the end — the end of our lives or the end of the world, whichever comes first."

Fred said, "I can see how faith in forgiveness is more important than believing six-day creation. But there is still some connection, isn't there?"

"Yes. There's a connection all right," Pastor Martin said. "The same God tells us both things. You can't trust somebody and not believe what he says. We trust God and we believe all that he says. But Satan attacks part of the Bible for the purpose of casting doubt on all of it. He wants to shake our faith in forgiveness. We are not strong enough to withstand his attacks on our own. We are left with nothing but to trust God. But that is good news, too, because God is trustworthy. He will not fail us."

23. The Man Who Worried About the Trinity

Read Matthew 28:18-20.

One Saturday morning Fred was sitting alone in the living room, reading the newspaper, and trying to motivate himself to get busy with one of the chores that were waiting for him around the house and the yard. Everyone else in the family was busy somewhere else, and Fred was not in much of a hurry to do anything. Then the doorbell rang, and Fred got up to see who was there.

At the door was a smiling, middle-aged man with a young child. The man said, "Hi! I want to ask you a question. Are you concerned about the spread of nuclear arms?"

Fred said, "What? Do you want me to sign some petition or something?"

"No," said the visitor. "We are just concerned about the things that are causing people anxiety these days. Don't you know that the spread of nuclear arms may mean that the end of the world is near? Doesn't that worry you?"

Fred said, "Let me guess. You're from the Jehovah's Witnesses, right?"

The visitor said, "Well, yes, as a matter of fact, we are Jehovah's Witnesses."

Fred went on, "You just want to use that question about nuclear arms to get around to your religious ideas on the end of the world and all that, right?"

The man said, "We do think that we can offer people hope from the Scriptures."

Fred was feeling confident. He had been in church and Bible class regularly. He thought he had learned a lot. He had heard Pastor Martin speak on the cult called Jehovah's Witnesses. He thought he could handle the situation. So he invited the visitor inside, with the young child. They introduced themselves and all sat down in the living room for a talk.

Fred figured that this was his home, so he could set the topic for discussion. He did not let the Jehovah's Witness take the initiative. So Fred said, "Listen, there's something I've been wanting to ask one of you Jehovah's Witnesses."

"What's that?" asked the visitor.

"Why don't you believe in the Trinity?" was Fred's question.

The man said, "The Trinity is just a human idea. History shows that it goes back to Greek philosophy, not the Bible. The Bible never uses the word 'triune' or the word 'Trinity.' It was Satan who used Greek philosophy at the Council of Nicea in the year 325 to take over the control of what were supposed to be Christian churches. That was the first time the Trinity was considered a Christian teaching."

"But, wait a minute," Fred objected. "The Trinity is, too, in the Bible."

The man said, "You can't show me one passage where the Bible uses the word 'Trinity' or the word 'triune.' "

Fred tried to think. He was about to say, "No, I guess I can't," when the visitor went on, "In fact, you can't show me any instance of any Christian talking about the Trinity before the year 325. That is hundreds of years after the Bible was written. So how can it be a Christian idea?

Besides, I know my arithmetic. One plus one plus one equals three — not one. If you believe in the Trinity, then you really believe in three gods, not in the one true God. But the Bible says there is only one true God."

Fred hemmed and hawed a bit. He had not expected such a torrential and well-rehearsed response from the man. Fred really did not have anything to say that he thought would be an adequate response. He finally said simply, "Look, I was baptized in the name of the Father and of the Son and of the Holy Ghost. That's three persons, one God, and that's the God I trust for salvation. And that's that."

Just then Leona came home from her shopping trip, and Fred explained that he had to help her unload the car. As an excuse it was a bit weak, but it got the unwanted visitor out the door.

After they had put the groceries away, Fred told Leona about the conversation. He was not happy about the result. Leona tried to comfort him by saying, "Remember, Fred, the pastor said that even people with a lot of experience dealing with the cults have trouble just getting those people to think. It's not a failure just on your part."

Fred said, "I know, Honey. You're right. But I can't help thinking that I should have had something better to say to him." Fred was worried. By this time, though, he knew better than to stew over any spiritual problem. He phoned the pastor right away. Pastor Martin had several other calls to make, but he promised to stop at Fred and Leona's place late in the afternoon.

Pastor Martin arrived just at the beginning of the climactic ninth inning of a baseball game that Fred and the children were watching on television. Fred asked whether the pastor would mind waiting a few minutes until the game was over. Pastor Martin suggested that he might even be persuaded to watch the end of the game with them.

After cheering their favorite team to a victory, Fred and the pastor settled into the living room. Leona joined them there for the discussion of the doctrine of the Trinity. First

Fred explained the interview with the Jehovah's Witness that morning. He explained again how incompetent he had felt when finally all he could do was to point out that he had been baptized in the name of the triune God.

Pastor Martin said, "The doctrine of the Trinity is really just the plain facts that the Bible presents. It tells us that there is only one God, for instance, where it says, 'The Lord our God is one Lord' (Deuteronomy 6:4). But the Bible says, too, that the Father is God. It talks about 'the God and Father of our Lord Jesus Christ' (1 Peter 1:3). The Bible says that the Son is God, for instance, when it says, 'In the beginning was the Word, and the Word was with God, and the Word was God' (John 1:1). And it says that the Holy Spirit is God, like when Peter said that a man named Ananias had lied to the Holy Ghost and that meant that he had lied to God (Acts 5:3,4)."

Leona said, "OK, Pastor. We believe that. But will a Jehovah's Witness listen, even if we say it that clearly?"

Pastor Martin responded, "Maybe and maybe not. They are, to some extent, brainwashed, you know. But the Holy Ghost will work through his word. We have that confidence, and with that confidence we can speak to these unbelievers. If they still do not believe, then it is their fault."

Fred asked, "But what can I say when this guy insists that the doctrine of the Trinity is just a philosophical theory? I mean, I can point out the biblical facts, but then he's gonna say that's nonsense. The man this morning said that one plus one plus one equals three, not one. So according to him I must worship more than one god. What do I say?"

Pastor Martin said, "There's no surefire answer if you mean to ask me what is going to convince him. I mean, they think they have surefire answers for every situation. It isn't that easy. But the best thing, as always, is just to tell the truth. Here the truth is that you are staying with the facts of the Bible and that he's the one who's being philosophical. He is the one who is using his mind to judge what is right and wrong in the Bible. And that's being philosophical, using the human mind to measure and judge all things.

"He may not admit it, but he is being philosophical and you are being biblical. Say that in so many words. It may not make much of an impression, but it just might make him think critically about what he's heard in the Jehovah's Witnesses circles."

Fred continued, "This man also said that the words 'triune' and 'Trinity' are not in the Bible. That doesn't seem very important to me, but I didn't know what to answer."

The pastor said, "If we were bound to the exact words the Bible uses, then we would have to talk about God only in Greek and Hebrew, the languages in which the Bible was written. These words are just a shorthand way of referring to the biblical fact that God is three persons, yet only one divine being. That's all."

"OK, Pastor," Fred said, "There's one more thing he said that I just didn't know how to answer. He said that there was no doctrine of the Trinity before some date several centuries after the New Testament was written. I didn't get that point."

Pastor Martin said, "He was probably referring to the year A.D. 325 and the Council of Nicea."

Fred said, "That's right. That's it."

The pastor went on, "In that year a large number of pastors did meet in the city of Nicea, which is in modern day Turkey. The situation was serious, for many people were denying the doctrine of the Trinity. These men confessed the biblical doctrine and put it into the first form of what we know as the Nicene Creed."

"Oh, that's it," said Fred.

Leona put in, "But that creed really says the same as the Apostle's Creed. It's just what the Bible teaches."

"Right," said the pastor, "and it is what Christians have taught since Bible times. But the Jehovah's Witnesses don't like the Nicene Creed — can't stand it — because it's so clear in saying that Jesus is true God. The Jehovah's Witnesses believe that he is really just a sort of super angel who became a man and then became an angel again."

Fred asked, "Can I show this to a Jehovah's Witness?"

Pastor Martin said, "You can show him these passages and see what he says. It takes the Holy Spirit to convince him of the truth."

Fred said, "It still seems a bit complicated to go through with somebody. Isn't there a simpler way to make the point, you know, something that might have more impact?"

Pastor Martin said, "Fred, you were so worried that you might not have said the right thing. I really think that you said about the best thing you could have said this morning when you referred to Jesus' command to baptize all nations 'in the name of Father, and of the Son, and of the Holy Ghost.' There you have Jesus himself naming the three persons of the Trinity. It won't do to say that these are just three names for God and not three persons. They are three persons because they are named separately and distinctly. And it won't do to say that only one of these persons is God and the others are not. If that were so, then Jesus would not speak of the name or revelation of God as including all three persons."

"So that's the answer after all," Fred was happy to note. "The doctrine of the Trinity was not something invented by philosophers. Jesus Himself taught it."

"That's right," said the pastor. "In fact, the Old Testament already taught this doctrine, from the very first page of Genesis. That's why when the angel Gabriel spoke to Zacharias and Mary at the beginning of Luke's Gospel, telling about the coming Messiah, he could refer to the three persons. And he was understood by Zacharias and Mary, who had had, after all, only the Old Testament."

Leona was bit upset. She said, "That's well and good. But is it going to do any good to win a debate with these Jehovah's Witnesses?"

Pastor Martin responded, "No, winning a debate is not the idea. It is too easy for us to get into that kind of thinking.

But I don't think that's what Fred is interested in, either. Actually, to prevent that, it is very good to use this passage about baptizing in the name of the triune God. That passage is about salvation, which is the practical interest here.

"The God who saves us is the triune God. The God we believe in and trust is the triune God. We have been baptized, washed from the guilt of our sins and brought to faith in Christ — we have been saved, in other words, by the triune God. The Father sent the Son to die on the cross bearing the guilt for all our sins and for the sins of the whole world. Our sins are forgiven for that reason. And the Father and the Son sent the Holy Spirit to work through the word and Holy Baptism and the Lord's Supper — to distribute forgiveness and salvation to us, to bring us to faith and then to keep us in the one true faith."

Fred said, "So I said the best thing after all, in a way, when I said that it was the Father, the Son, and the Holy Spirit that I believed in and trusted for my salvation."

"I think so," said the pastor. "In fact, I'm sure of it. What else is there to talk about anyway."

"And not only that," said Leona, "but that means that if they claim to trust in Christ but do not believe that he is true God, then they have faith in someone they don't believe to be God. They should admit that they must be worshipping an idol."

"Good point," said the pastor. "We trust the triune God because he is the one true God, the God revealed in the Bible, the God Who has saved us. We believe in the real Jesus Christ, the Christ we learn about in Scripture. Otherwise we would be lost. And the only purpose in speaking up for the doctrine of the Trinity is to tell others about the salvation that God the Son earned by dying on the cross, the salvation that God the Holy Ghost assures us about through word and sacrament."

24. The Man Who Worried About Prestige

Read Matthew 20:20-28.

Fred went through a very rough period in the office where he worked. There was quite a shuffle in jobs and responsibilities and the whole structure of the company. Fred or any other worker might have lost his job. But then, there were also opportunities. Fred or any other worker might have gotten a promotion with a big raise.

Some of the people in the office were demoralized, but most of them just worked all the harder. Fred worked a lot of extra hours, paid special attention to details in every aspect of his work, and in general tried to make himself indispensable to the company.

In the scramble to get a better job or just to keep one's own job, there developed quite a campaign of office politics. Everyone was talking behind everyone else's back. People tried to show each other up. The salesmen were fighting over territories and routes and customers and expense accounts. The people whose jobs kept them in the office were always trying to be seen with the right superiors — or to be seen by them doing the right thing at the right time.

Fred was not happy with this period in his career. He did not like the way this competition made him feel. But he was thinking about the things he and Leona wanted to buy. He was thinking about education for the children. Indirectly, Leona and the children put a lot of pressure on Fred. Fred wanted to be "somebody."

Even if Leona had the best of intentions in building him up, complimenting him, expressing her confidence that he was and would continue to be a good provider — even then she was unintentionally putting a lot of pressure on him. Fred got the idea that it was awfully important to Leona, too, that he come out on top in this scramble at the office.

Fred even got involved in the office politics. He did not like himself for it, and he tried to stay out of it. But he noticed more and more how his comments and actions in the office were dominated by the desire to beat out the other guy and get a certain promotion. For a time his job became the most important thing in his life. For a time his job cut into the time he normally spent on family and church activities. He lost a lot of sleep.

When all was said and done — and a lot more was said than done — it was clear that things would settle down in the company. It was also clear that Fred had ended up in the same place he had started out. He had the same job, the same salary with a cost of living adjustment, perhaps a little more job security, and a new boss, the man he had hoped to beat out for the higher job. Fred now had to concentrate on keeping this former rival happy with him. Fred had to eat some humble pie and concentrate on doing his job day by day again. It was a tough adjustment in one way, but in another way it was a relief. He was glad the scramble was over.

But Fred was a bit disappointed with himself, and he correctly sensed that Leona was also a bit disappointed. But, much more than Fred, she was relieved that the pressure was off for a while. Yet late one Friday evening, Fred and Leona were sitting and watching television. After the late news, Leona turned to Fred and said, "Why so glum, chum?"

Fred said, "Oh, I don't know."

Leona answered, "I think maybe you could make a good guess. How about a glass of milk and we'll talk about it?"

So they sat at the dining room table and ate some cookies and drank some milk. Slowly and gradually Fred admitted to Leona that he was disappointed about not getting the promotion and that he was disappointed in himself for having cared too much and having tried in the wrong way to get the promotion. Finally he admitted that he was also worried that she might be disappointed in him. He said, "Maybe it's that old male ego, but no man wants his wife to consider him a failure."

Leona patted his hand and said, "Fred, you're not a failure. You're a good husband and a good father — and that's more important than any career. You've still got your job. And even if you aren't proud of everything you've said or done lately, you were still a Christian battling with temptation. It wasn't like you had given in to it totally."

"That's true," said Fred. "God did not let me fall away. A Christian is always battling with temptation in this life. If the battle stops in this life, it's because the person has given up on the Christian faith."

"Besides," said Leona, "I've learned something myself lately, and I've been wanting to share it with you."

"What's that?" asked her husband.

Leona told him this story: "You know that I worked pretty closely with Pastor Martin and some of the ladies at church on Vacation Bible School last week. Pastor Martin taught a youth class. The rest of us were teaching school children.

"One afternoon we adults were talking after most of the kids had gone home. I told them about two boys in my class who were really arguing with each other about who was stronger. One said he could lift a horse. The other said he could lift an elephant, and so on and so forth."

Fred interjected, "Really childish — just like office politics."

Leona said, "I was thinking at the time that it was really childish. But Pastor Martin pointed out that only the things they were saying were childish. The pride and the rivalry are problems for all of us all our lives. He pointed out that in a few years those boys would still be trying to prove the same thing, only they would do it by competing in sports and then later still by competing in professions. We are always tending to be proud and full of rivalry."

"Well," said Fred, "I guess that makes me feel a little better, knowing that it isn't just my problem."

"But there's more," said Leona. "I told Pastor Martin about some of my dreams that never came true, you know, like my dream of being a world-famous concert pianist or a world-famous anything. I told him I sometimes felt cheated or ashamed that, when I was younger, I didn't have the drive or the courage to risk everything on the chance that I could make it big in one of those fields. You know what he said?"

"No, what?"

"Pastor Martin said that God was pleased with my teaching Vacation Bible School for a few days — if I did it to honor him and for the salvation of the children's souls — but God would not be at all pleased with even the greatest career in any field if I did it for my own glory and fame."

"Did that help you?" Fred asked.

"Yes, it did," said his wife. "I realized that he was right and that it would be better to please God, even with something the world thinks is child's play, than to have everybody except God applauding."

"If I know Pastor Martin," said Fred, "he must have backed that up with something from the Bible."

"Yes, he did," said Leona. She got out their family Bible and showed him Matthew 20:20-28. They were especially struck by Jesus' words that any one who wanted to be great among Christians should be a servant.

Fred said, "Well, I know I've said this before, but I sure have been barking up the wrong tree. I wasn't using my job as an opportunity to serve people and honor God. I was using it mostly just to glorify myself and get ahead, even at the expense of other people. I have to admit, that's pretty sinful."

Leona hastened to comfort her husband, "Yes, but remember the last passage in this section: 'Even as the Son of man came not to be ministered unto, but to minister, and to give his life a ransom for many.' We always have to keep that in mind. Christ was the greatest servant of all."

Fred thought about that, and then he said, "It's curious. That passage presents Christ as the greatest servant, the perfect example of the kind of self-sacrificing people we should all be. Of course, that is hard for us to hear because we know we don't measure up. But at the same time, that passage speaks about forgiveness for sins like pride and rivalry and jockeying for position at the expense of others. Right there Jesus was forgiving the apostles for their pride."

Leona summed it all up, "Christ died for all our sins, so he must have died for this sin, too."

Fred said, "And that means that our sins are forgiven. We always have a new start in Christ — and new motivation to follow his example."

Leona said, "Something else comes to me out of all this, Fred."

"What's that?"

"Even good works aren't good works if we do them to earn credit with God," she said. "An employee who is only out for his own good is hardly an example of loyalty to the company or friendship to the boss. He is just serving himself."

Fred completed the thought, "Yeah. I think the pastor was trying to say that in a sermon a couple of weeks ago. A good work is really a good work only if it's done for the purpose of glorifying God and helping other people, if it is really done from God-given love. We aren't God's employees at all. We are God's children for Jesus' sake. Jesus has done it all, earned everything we need, including forgiveness and salvation. We don't serve God for the sake of reward. We serve God out of gratitude, for the sake of love, moved by all that he has done for us in Christ."

By then it was getting late. Fred and Leona decided to call it a night and get some sleep. Fred's mind was greatly eased, and he slept better that night than he had for months. Although he was very sleepy, he still tried to read a psalm before going to sleep. But he just could not keep his eyes open. He was reading Psalm 127 but fell asleep just after reading the second verse: "It is vain for you to rise up early, to sit up late, to eat the bread of sorrows: for so he giveth his beloved sleep."

25. The Man Who Did Not Worry About Dying

Read Romans 8:31-39.

One day Fred collapsed at work. He was rushed to the hospital by ambulance. It was discovered that he had had a mild heart attack. He was admitted to the coronary care unit, where his heart's functions were monitored constantly by those beeping machines. He would have to undergo several tests before it could be decided what treatment he should have and what, medically speaking, the prospect was for returning to an active life.

Any illness reminds a person that he is mortal and will someday die, unless Jesus returns first. A heart attack is perhaps the biggest such reminder there is. The heart attack also created other concerns. It was hard for Leona to see her husband confined to bed and hooked up to the monitors. She and Ned, their teenaged son, were the only family members permitted by hospital rules to visit him. And only brief visits were permitted at that. It was very hard to explain the whole situation to the younger children.

Leona was worried. Her worries were not mainly financial. Fred had been a conscientious provider. Leona had a career to fall back on. Most importantly, Leona remembered that God was trustworthy and would take care of her and her family no matter what happened. Leona's worries were more personal. She did not want to be without Fred. But she knew that God could and would help her even then.

Fred was not worried. Pastor Martin visited him nearly every day and saw no signs that Fred was worried. He told the pastor one day, "I'm not worried at all. I know that God will make things turn out for the best."

The pastor agreed, "That's right!"

"I really mean it!" Fred went on. "I can't lose. If I die, I go to be with the Lord. If I live, he'll be with me here. So I really can't lose on that score. The only bad thing would be leaving the family behind. But God can even make that work out for the best somehow."

Pastor Martin observed, "Fred, as long as I've known you, you've been a worrier. Now, at a time when most people would be scared stiff, you're not worried at all."

Fred chuckled, "Maybe I've finally learned something."

Fred did not want to die. He prayed often, alone or with the pastor or with Leona and Ned, that he would be spared so that he could be with the family and serve God yet more and more with a longer life. But he always prayed with the knowledge that God knew what was best. He prayed, "Thy will be done."

After Fred had been in the hospital several days and had undergone more tests than he thought possible, a specialist told him that he needed open-heart surgery. The operation was dangerous. Fred might die on the operating table. With or without the operation, the doctor would offer no medical guarantees. Either way Fred might live for some time. Either way he might die soon and suddenly. But, weighing all the probabilities, the specialist recommended surgery.

146

That seemed to him to offer the best chance for Fred to return to an active life.

Fred got a second opinion. The other specialist agreed in recommending surgery. Fred and Leona talked about it. They realized that, with or without surgery, it was simply another time when they would have to trust God entirely. They woud have to make a careful decision and then leave the outcome in God's hands. Finally they decided to take the doctors' advice. Arrangements were made to have the operation as soon as possible.

That evening Leona phoned Pastor Martin to tell him about the operation. Pastor Martin comforted Leona with the truths of God's wisdom, love, mercy, and especially with a word about God's grace in Christ, the full and free forgiveness of all our sins. Pastor Martin said, "God didn't spare his own Son but had him crucified for the forgiveness of our sins. If he loves us that much, then he will certainly direct all other events for our benefit." Pastor Martin promised to visit Fred the next day in the hospital.

He drove over to see Fred the next afternoon. Driving in the car, walking in from the parking lot, riding the elevator, the pastor kept wondering exactly what he would say to Fred. Only a short visit was permitted in the coronary care unit anyway. Pastor Martin only hoped to bring Fred one more message from the word of God to strengthen his faith in the love and grace of Christ, no matter what might happen.

As it turned out, the pastor did not get to do much talking. He found Fred in a happy mood. After exchanging pleasantries and the basic information about Fred's condition, Fred had something to tell the pastor. This is the story he told:

"Pastor, late last night they brought a man in. He'd had a pretty severe heart attack, I guess, and it wasn't his first, either. He had a lot of medication in him, so we didn't talk at all last night. But this morning we were both awake at the same time for a while. He wanted to talk.

"He was scared stiff. I think he would have had an easier time with his heart except that he was so afraid of dying. I really felt sorry for him. I guess I could understand what he was feeling.

"But, you know, he couldn't understand me. First he thought maybe I didn't have anything really wrong with my heart and maybe I'd be going home soon. I told him that I needed a pretty serious operation. He was amazed that I wasn't scared stiff just like him.

"Then he decided that I must just be the kind of guy who never worries about anything. I told him that wasn't so. I'd had my share of worries. He just couldn't understand why I wasn't afraid of dying.

"So I just told him that I wasn't afraid of dying because of Jesus Christ. I told him that because of what Jesus did for me I knew I was going to heaven whenever I might die. Meanwhile, I knew that Jesus would be with me and help me out with whatever I would have to face in this life.

"Well, he wanted to know more. But he was pretty tired and didn't have a lot of energy or attention. So I just got out my Bible and read him something that I had just read myself a little while before."

Fred got out his Bible again and turned to Romans 8. He read for the pastor verses 33 and 34: "Who shall lay any thing to the charge of God's elect? It is God that justifieth. Who is he that condemneth? It is Christ that died, yea rather, that is risen again, who is even at the right hand of God, who also maketh intercession for us."

Then Fred went on with the story: "So I just told this gentleman that God had forgiven my sins and declared me not guilty because of the death of Jesus Christ. I told him that Jesus, the Son of God, became a man to bear all our sins himself and to suffer in our place on the cross. He died for our sins, and he rose from the dead to show our sins forgiven. And with our sins forgiven, there is nothing that can keep us out of heaven. I told him that I knew if I died

148

today or tomorrow or whenever, I would be with the Lord Jesus in Paradise right away.

"And, you know, Pastor, the most wonderful thing happened. I looked over at him and I saw tears in his eyes. He told me that he had been raised a Christian but it had been years since he had heard those words about Christ and about forgiveness of sins for Jesus' sake. He told me that hearing what I read from the word of God brought back faith that he had long since forgotten about. He told me he wasn't so worried anymore. He told me that he wanted to be with Jesus, whom he had known as a child but had forgotten as a man until this morning."

Pastor Martin had known all along that the other bed in Fred's room was empty. Fred saw the pastor eyeing that bed. Pastor Martin asked, "And where is this fellow now?"

Fred said, "I have pretty good reason to hope that he's with the Lord Jesus right now, don't you think?"

The pastor agreed. Then it was time for him to leave. He said a short prayer and they joined in the Lord's Prayer. Then Pastor Martin left with a promise to come back the next day to give Fred private communion.

When Pastor Martin came back to the hospital the next day, he was wondering again what he was going to say to Fred. It seemed that Fred did not need much comforting. Instead, he was himself dispensing comfort from the word of God. As it turned out, the pastor did not have to do much talking that day either. After a quiet but joyous private communion, Fred had another story to tell, and this is what he said:

"Pastor, the strangest thing happened a little while ago. Some guy came in here and introduced himself as the Protestant chaplain at the hospital. I don't know what denomination he was from, but I didn't mind talking with him if he had the time.

"Well, he said some of the weirdest things I could imagine a chaplain saying to someone who's really sick. First off, he tells me how good the doctors and nurses at this hospital are. I told him that I was sure they were all very fine but that I was trusting God.

"Then he goes on about how good my chances are to get better. I told him that I didn't need that kind of talk. I said I knew that I might die and I wasn't in any mood to ignore that possibility. He didn't want to face that, I guess.

"Anyway, then he goes on to say that he hoped that I had had a full life and that, in the unlikely event that I would 'pass away,' I could be assured that there would be many people who would have good and happy memories of me.

"I told him I knew that there were people who would be glad that I'd been around. But I asked him why he didn't talk to me about heaven and hell, about Jesus who had saved me from hell and was going to take me to heaven.

"This guy calls himself a chaplain, and you know what he said? He said modern man was too sophisticated or something to believe in heaven and hell anymore. The only afterlife would be living on in other people's memories.

"At that point I told him to hold the phone, and I got out my Bible. In fact, I read to him from Romans 8 again, the same chapter I showed you yesterday."

Then Fred got out his Bible again and read for the pastor Romans 8:37-39: "Nay, in all these things we are more than conquerors through him that loved us. For I am persuaded that neither death, nor life, nor angels, nor principalities, nor powers, nor things present, nor things to come, nor height, nor depth, nor any other creature, shall be able to separate us from the love of God, which is in Christ Jesus our Lord."

Fred laid the Bible down open on his lap. He looked up at the pastor and said, "I told that so-called chaplain that he didn't know the first thing about God if he thought that God would be through loving me when I died. I told him that not death, not anything could separate me from the love of God in Christ. I told him that if the old ticker gives out today or if I don't wake up from the surgery tomorrow, the angels were going to carry me up to heaven, just like

Jesus tells about the beggar Lazarus. In my spirit I'm just a poor beggar, too. But I'm saved by the death and resurrection of Jesus Christ my Lord."

Pastor Martin asked, "What did he have to say to that?"

Fred said, "I don't remember. I don't think he had much of anything to say. He gave me a strange look when he left, as if I had told him I believed in some fairy tale or something."

The pastor said, "It's sad, but some people do think that the truth is only a fairy tale."

Pastor Martin prayed with Fred and then left. Fred's operation was scheduled for the next morning. Pastor Martin was at the hospital early to say another prayer with Fred and Leona. He planned to wait at the hospital with Leona to find out the results of the surgery.

Fred thanked the pastor for coming and saying the prayer. He squeezed Leona's hand and told her not to worry. He was not worried in the least, he assured her. Then they wheeled Fred into the operating room. When the anesthetist put the mask over Fred's face, Fred was thinking about Jesus.